# SEEDS

By Ross Mackintosh

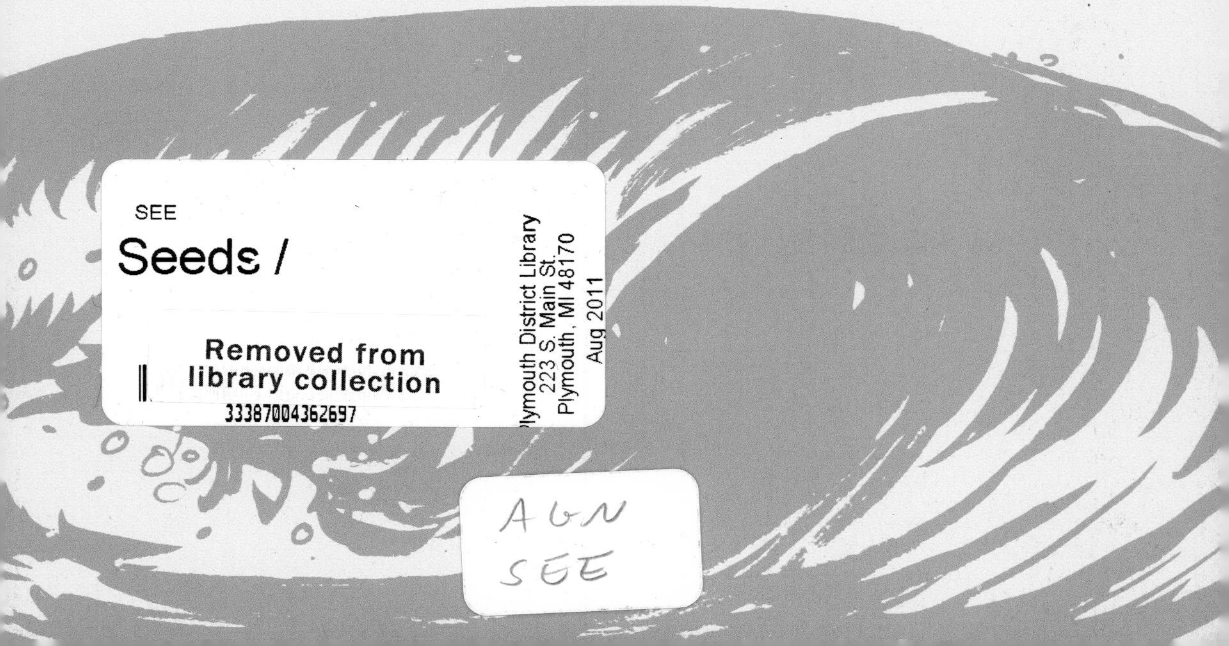

# FOREWORD (I)

Cartooning is the art of distilling reality to its essence. There is nothing superfluous in a good cartoon. That quality makes the medium particularly well-suited for memoir: comics are like memories, in that they filter and capture only the most important details. The difference between good and bad cartooning is how well the cartoonist filters and captures. Ross Mackintosh is a good cartoonist.

In the century-plus history of modern comics, the notion of using the medium to tell personal, powerful, true stories is relatively new. In Seeds, Mackintosh draws himself struggling to describe the type of "adult comic" he wants to attempt, not even sure what to call it. There are many people who still believe that comics are only meant to be funny ephemera for children. They are wrong. Seeds adds to a growing bibliography of comics work that refutes them with intelligence, maturity, sensitivity, seriousness of purpose, and wit.

Comics combine words and art to transcend the sum of their parts. Their lack of detail encourages readers to fill the void with details from their own lives and identify with abstract squiggles of ink. It's strange and wonderful. Readers will tell a cartoonist, "My family and situation were nothing at all like yours but it's as if you were sitting in our home watching us!" When this happens to Ross, as it will, he should graciously say thanks, take the credit, and not try to solve the paradox. He will have discovered that he has told a nearly universal story and that families facing a crisis are pretty much the same everywhere. It is a simultaneously sad and heartening realisation.

Having learned that lesson first-hand, I'm gratified but not surprised to recognise aspects of myself and my family in a story created by a man I've never met who lives a continent and an ocean away. Seeds is about Ross Mackintosh's family, and mine, and millions of others. That's what good comics can do.

Brian Fies
*Creator - Mom's Cancer*

# FOREWORD (II)

Death is part of life and comes to us all. Sometimes it is sudden and unexpected and at other times it announces itself well beforehand... but in both cases it is a subject which we still find difficult to talk about openly.

We all have to cope with the death of someone close to us in our lives - frequently this will be the death of a parent, though for a child it may also be the death of a cat or some other pet. What we need to do is be able to talk about it with someone we know well - either the person dying themselves or with friends, parents some other close confidante.

If we can discuss it with our nearest and dearest it helps both the dying and those left behind - to (a) come to terms with death (b) to know what the person dying and those who have to cope with the death - want.

As far as what the person who is dying actually wants - some will want lots of medical treatment to keep them alive as long as possible, whilst others will feel, because of the chances of treatment doing any good being so small - that they want the emphasis to be more on a 'dignified' death which is quick and as painless as  possible - but a kind of death where they feel 'in control'.

Seeing how Ross felt about his father's death will help others in the same situation.

Dr Ann McPherson FRCGP FRCP CBE, GP
*Medical Director of Health Experiences Research Group at University of Oxford.*
and

Dr Aidan Macfarlane MA, MBBCHir. FRCP, FRPCH, FFPH.
*Independent International Consultant in Child and Adolescent Health.*

# INTRODUCTION

My previous attempts at creating a comic story had always resulted in short, comedic sketches. I thought that if I were capable of creating a comic I would have to channel a more grand inspiration. This was to come sooner than I thought, and in a way I could not have predicted.

I often feel that I am observing my life, as if each overheard conversation or view of a scene is framed in my mind as a work of art. As the distressing events of my Dad's terminal disease unfolded, I couldn't help but visualise them as a sequence of images, narrated by my new opinions.

When dramatic things happen in our lives our senses amplify and we suddenly seem to have a more efficient memory. I wrote down snippets of dialogue and narration, without a clue of what I should do with them, but when I realised this could be a comic, I could see the whole thing in my mind, from beginning to end.

I worked on rough sketches between February and April 2010. I then spent three months pencilling and another three inking and lettering. I didn't presume anyone else would like to read it, let alone publish. As I was creating it, it became clear that it was not only a catharsis but somehow a gift for the casualties: my brothers and my Mom; a record of the tumult and a brief homage to my Dad. A way of prolonging the memory. A lot of work we do in life is done to achieve longevity, making our artifacts mimic our genes and live on after we depart.

From an early age we become aware that one day we will die, but are encouraged not to contemplate it. Indeed, mythologies have been created to distract us from it. All the people around us, our loved ones, our work colleagues, our bus drivers and celebrities, will end, just as we will. Although our instinctive self-preservation may find the prospect of decay and ultimate disappearance discomforting, it will happen. Should the consideration and discussion of an inevitable event in all our lives be so repulsive? Can't we all learn from hearing the opinions of others about something so pertinent? There's a reason that skeletons are used as figures of fear. It's not as if a ligament-free bone man can cause us any harm, is it? Think of Dickens' Ghost of Christmas Yet To Come, the thing that we fear the most. It's not a werewolf or an unpaid debt, it's death. Death and insignificance.

But this is not a book about death. It's a book about my Dad. A man who never took things too seriously. He was an engineer by trade, gradually working hard enough over the years to carve himself a niche whereby he could earn a living wage by exerting the least possible amount of effort. His love of sport was something he failed to pass on to his sons, but I can see how his curiosity about how things work (usually machinery) has passed on to me. It's unlikely Socrates' claim that, "The unexamined life is not worth living", was a conscious pursuit for Dad, but he certainly didn't like to take things at face value. His apparent working-class roots and pub-going, sport-loving image were at odds with his philosophical, inquisitive mind.

Dad was also a fan of comedy. Whether it was an Edinburgh Fringe stand-up or a new TV sit-com, Dad knew about it. He didn't enjoy fiction, be it literary or cinematic, preferring documentary – 'real life'. I'm not sure what he would have felt about being the main character in a 'factual' comic book but I'm certain he wouldn't disapprove.

Too many father/son relationships burst at the seams with unarticulated emotion and one can guess the reasons for this. My connection with my Dad, albeit still fraught with unspeak, was as satisfying as I could ask for.

Dad's care during the early stages of his decline was provided by an NHS Hospital. We are fortunate that we live in a country and period in history where we have doctors and nurses who are available to draw upon immense knowledge, gathered over centuries, and not only tell us what ails us but try their best to treat it. Overgate Hospice, who provided care in the later stages of Dad's illness, not only ensured my Dad was cared for in a sympathetic way, but the support they provide for families is nothing short of remarkable. That such an organisation exists within our society should reassure us all of the level of humanity we are capable of.

I am lucky. Some people experience the death of loved ones who haven't yet reached adulthood. I didn't. Some people don't get advance notice. I did.


Ross Mackintosh, 2011.

For Andy, Greg and Mom

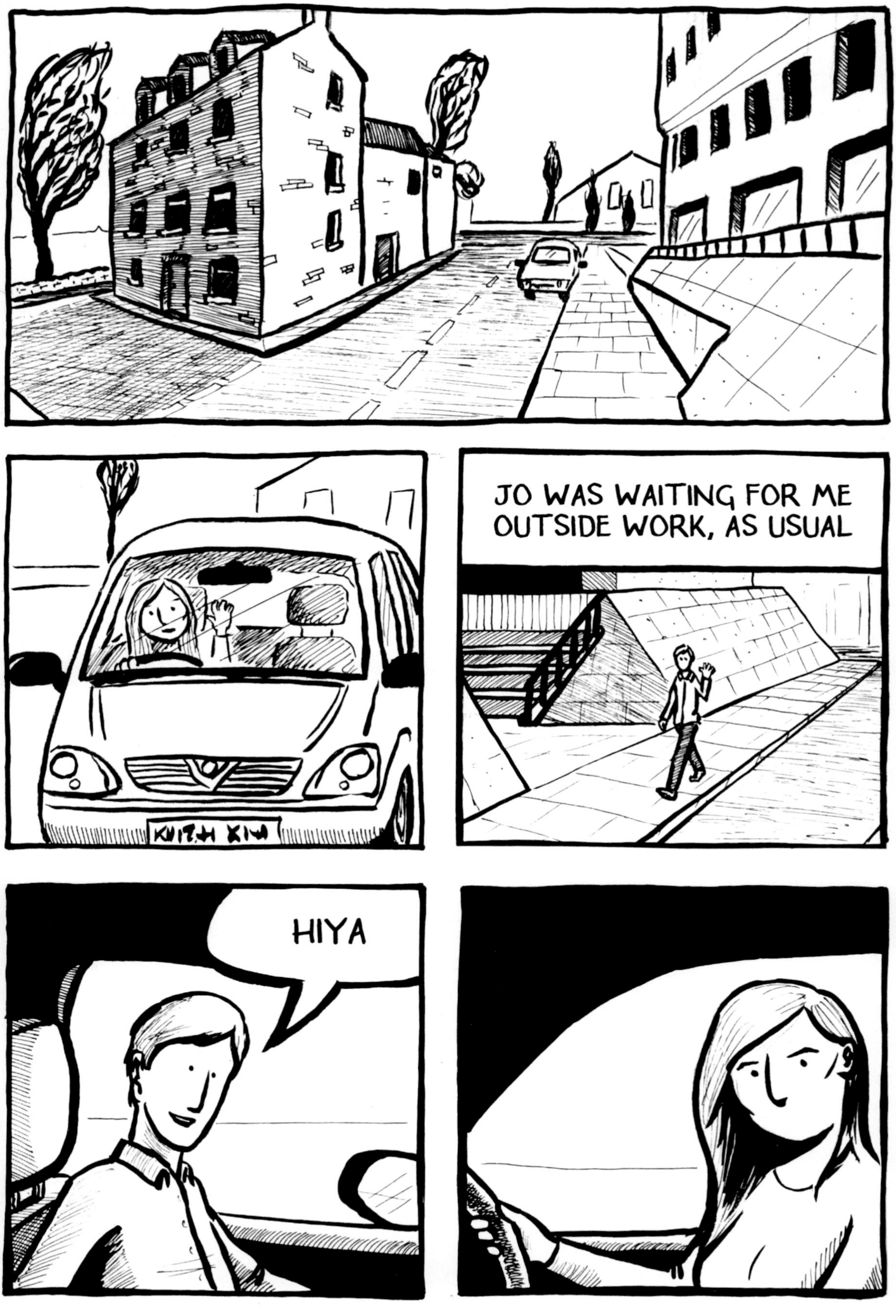
JO WAS WAITING FOR ME OUTSIDE WORK, AS USUAL
HIYA

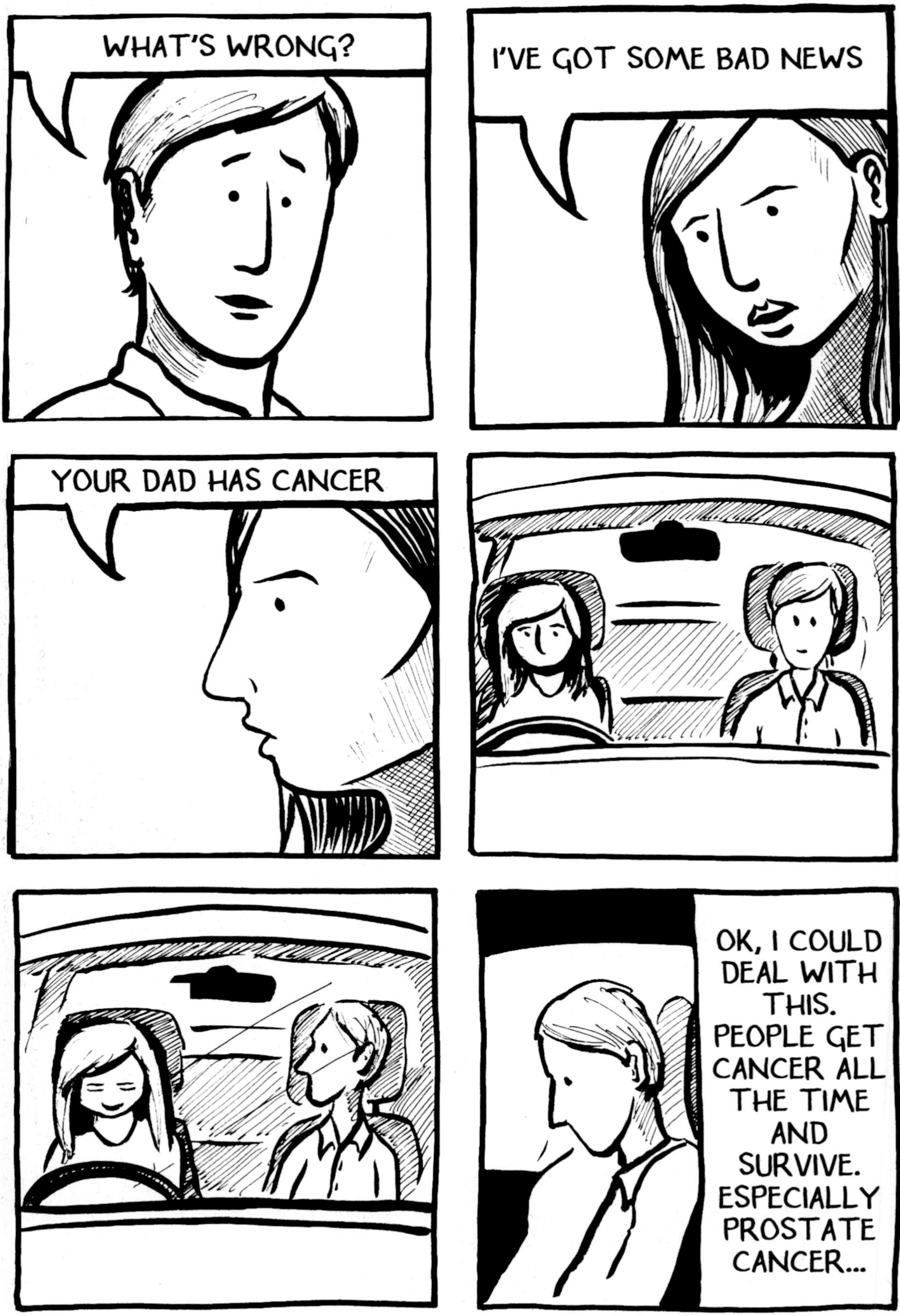
WHAT'S WRONG?
I'VE GOT SOME BAD NEWS
YOUR DAD HAS CANCER
OK, I COULD DEAL WITH THIS. PEOPLE GET CANCER ALL THE TIME AND SURVIVE. ESPECIALLY PROSTATE CANCER...

...AND THE GOOD NEWS WAS THAT THEY'D FOUND IT

DAD HAD HEALTH SCARES BEFORE...

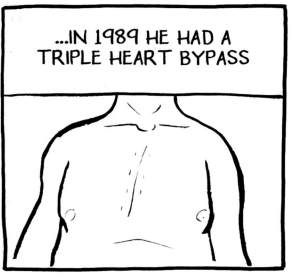

...IN 1989 HE HAD A TRIPLE HEART BYPASS

HE'S SPENT THE LAST DECADE OR SO TINKERING WITH HIS COMPUTER...

...OR WATCHING TV. HE RARELY LEFT HOME...

...AND WAS PERFECTLY HAPPY WITH THAT

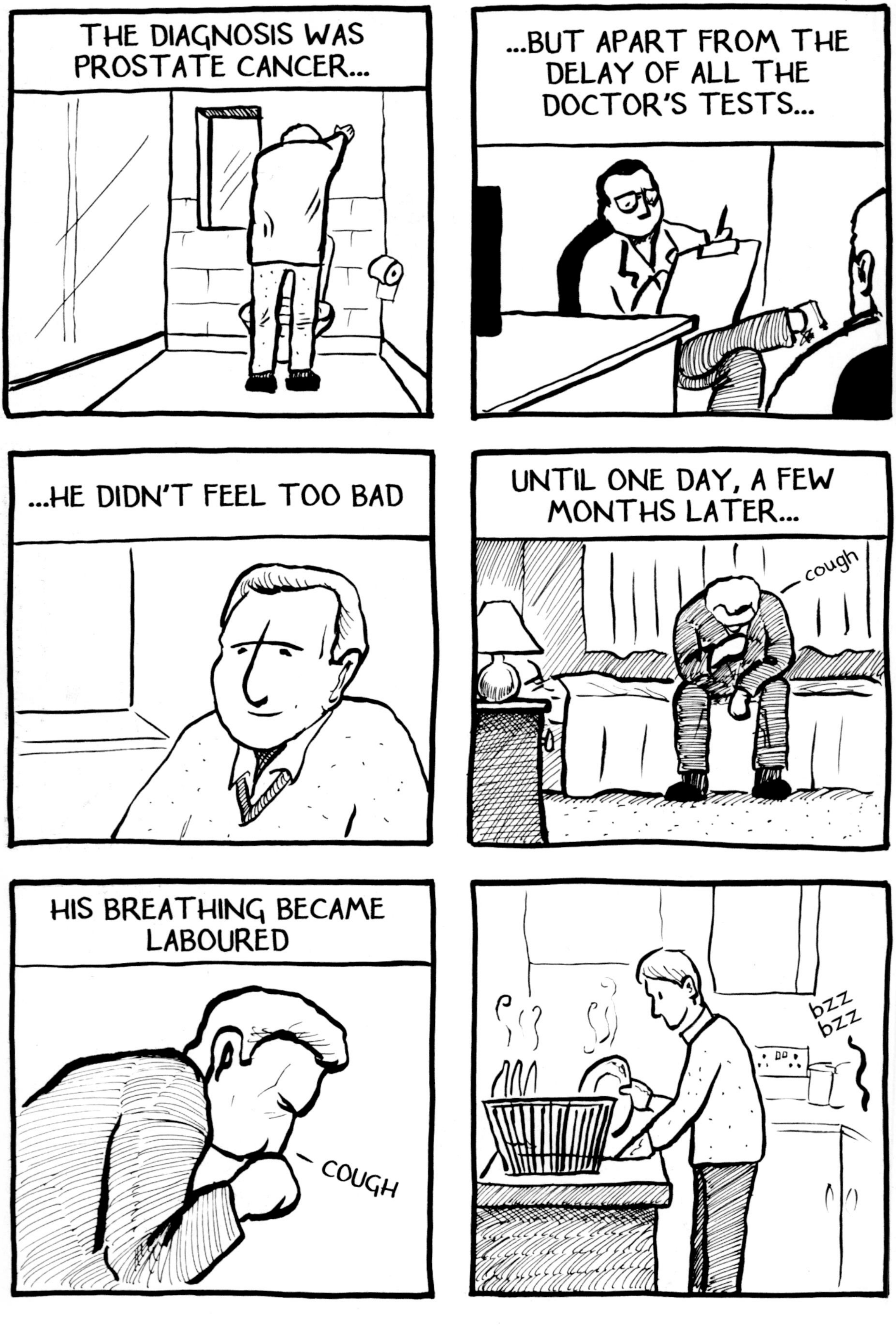
THE DIAGNOSIS WAS PROSTATE CANCER...
...BUT APART FROM THE DELAY OF ALL THE DOCTOR'S TESTS...
...HE DIDN'T FEEL TOO BAD
UNTIL ONE DAY, A FEW MONTHS LATER...
cough
HIS BREATHING BECAME LABOURED
COUGH
bzz bzz

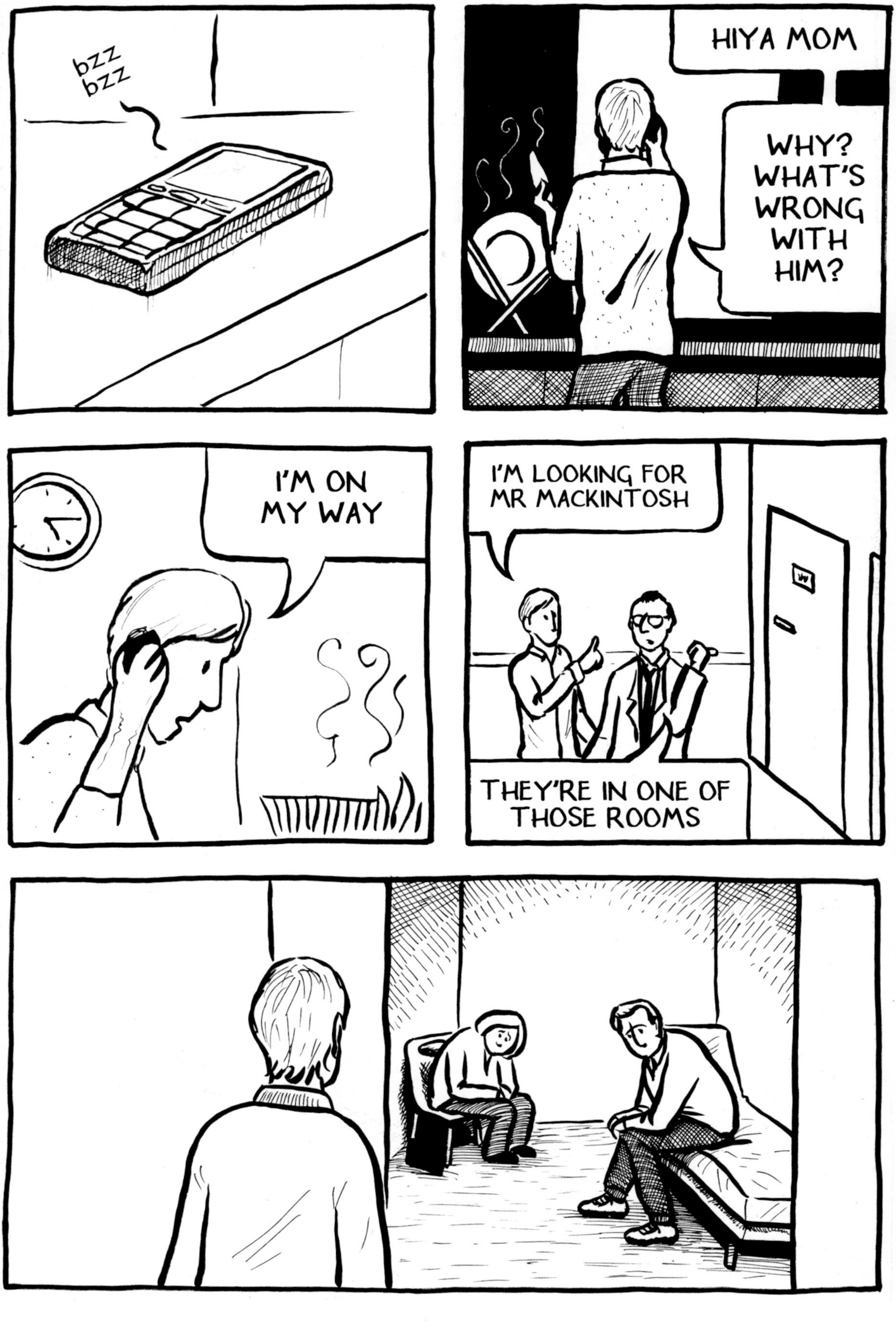
bzz
bzz
HIYA MOM
WHY? WHAT'S WRONG WITH HIM?
I'M ON MY WAY
I'M LOOKING FOR MR MACKINTOSH
THEY'RE IN ONE OF THOSE ROOMS

**DAD WAS CRYING**

**I'D NEVER SEEN HIM CRY**

**MOM TOLD ME THAT HE'D COME FOR A CHECK-UP ON HIS BREATHING, AND ENDED UP HYPERVENTILATING**

**THEY THINK IT WAS A PANIC ATTACK**

**AT LEAST I COULD NOW PUT MY ARM AROUND HIM**

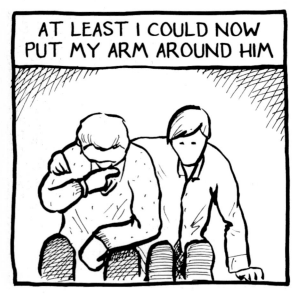

**..WHICH WAS SOMETHING I'D NEVER DONE BEFORE**

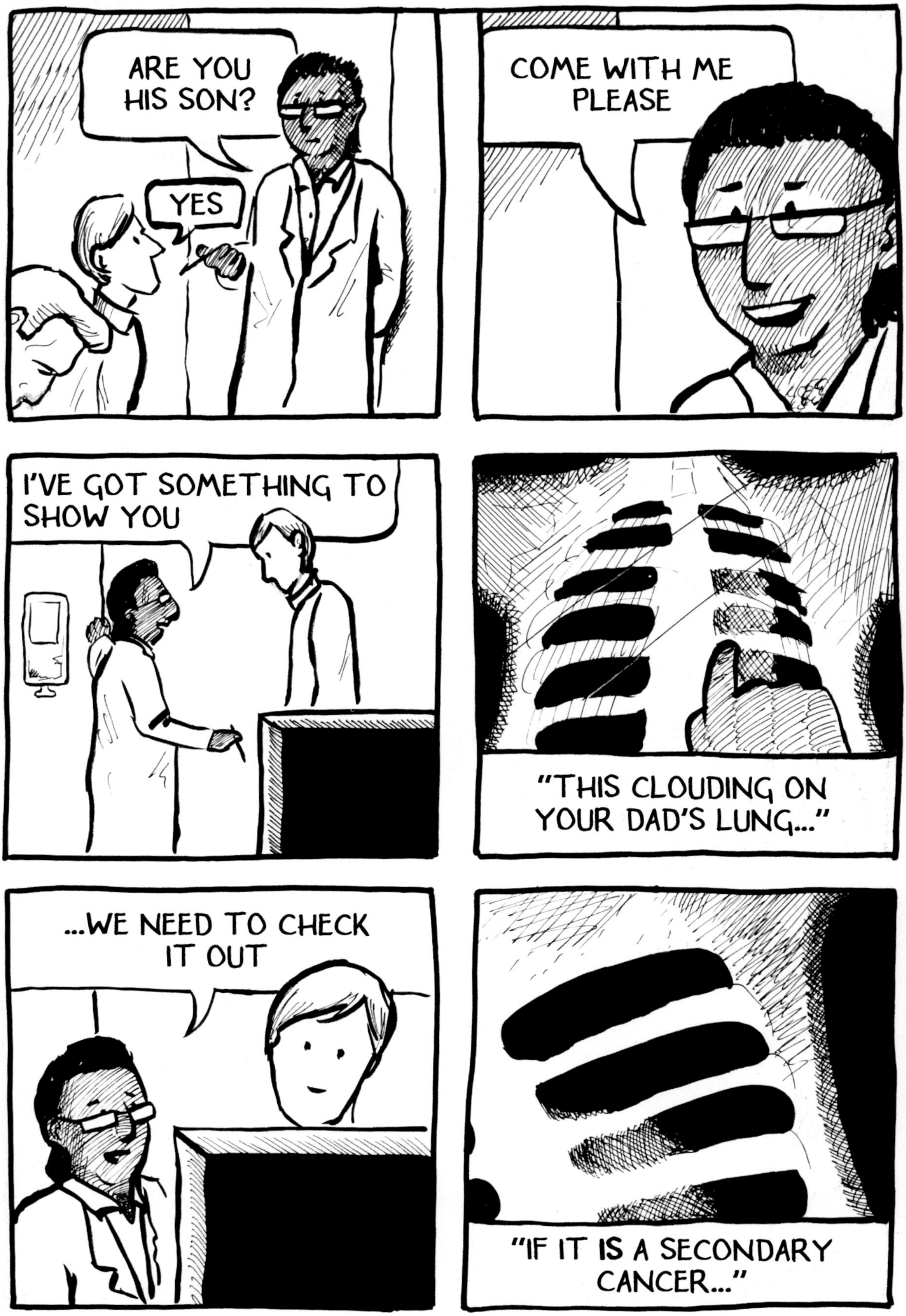
ARE YOU HIS SON?
YES
COME WITH ME PLEASE
I'VE GOT SOMETHING TO SHOW YOU
"THIS CLOUDING ON YOUR DAD'S LUNG..."
...WE NEED TO CHECK IT OUT
"IF IT IS A SECONDARY CANCER..."

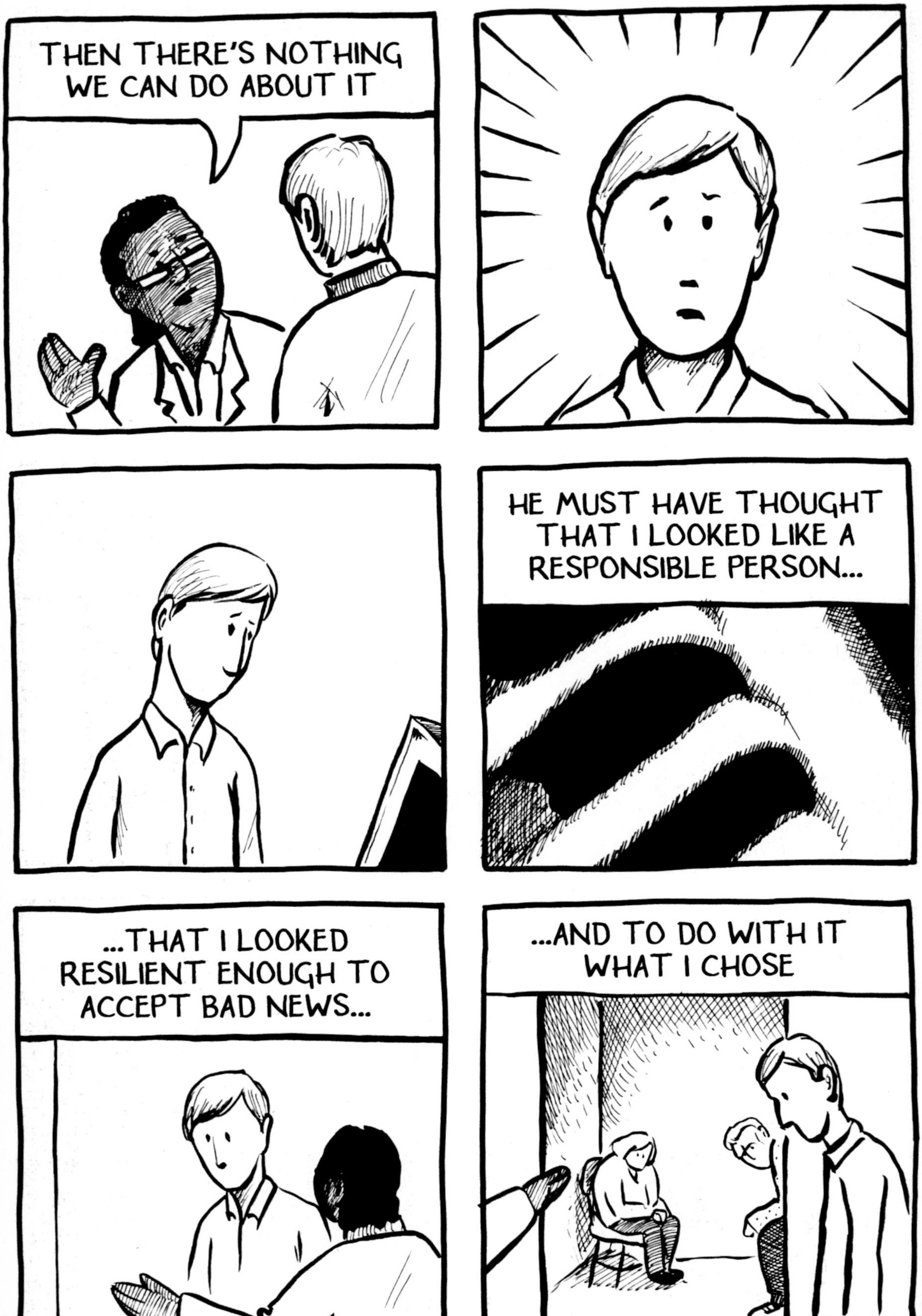
THEN THERE'S NOTHING WE CAN DO ABOUT IT
HE MUST HAVE THOUGHT THAT I LOOKED LIKE A RESPONSIBLE PERSON...
...THAT I LOOKED RESILIENT ENOUGH TO ACCEPT BAD NEWS...
...AND TO DO WITH IT WHAT I CHOSE

WHAT WAS I GOING TO TELL THEM?

I GUESS THEY HAD WORKED IT OUT FOR THEMSELVES

WE'LL NEED TO KEEP HIM IN HOSPITAL OVERNIGHT

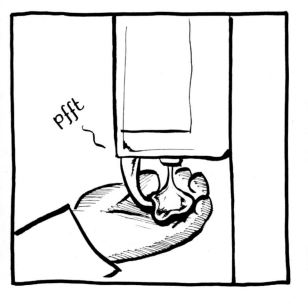

A PORTER WILL BE HERE SOON

HE'LL TAKE YOUR DAD TO A WARD

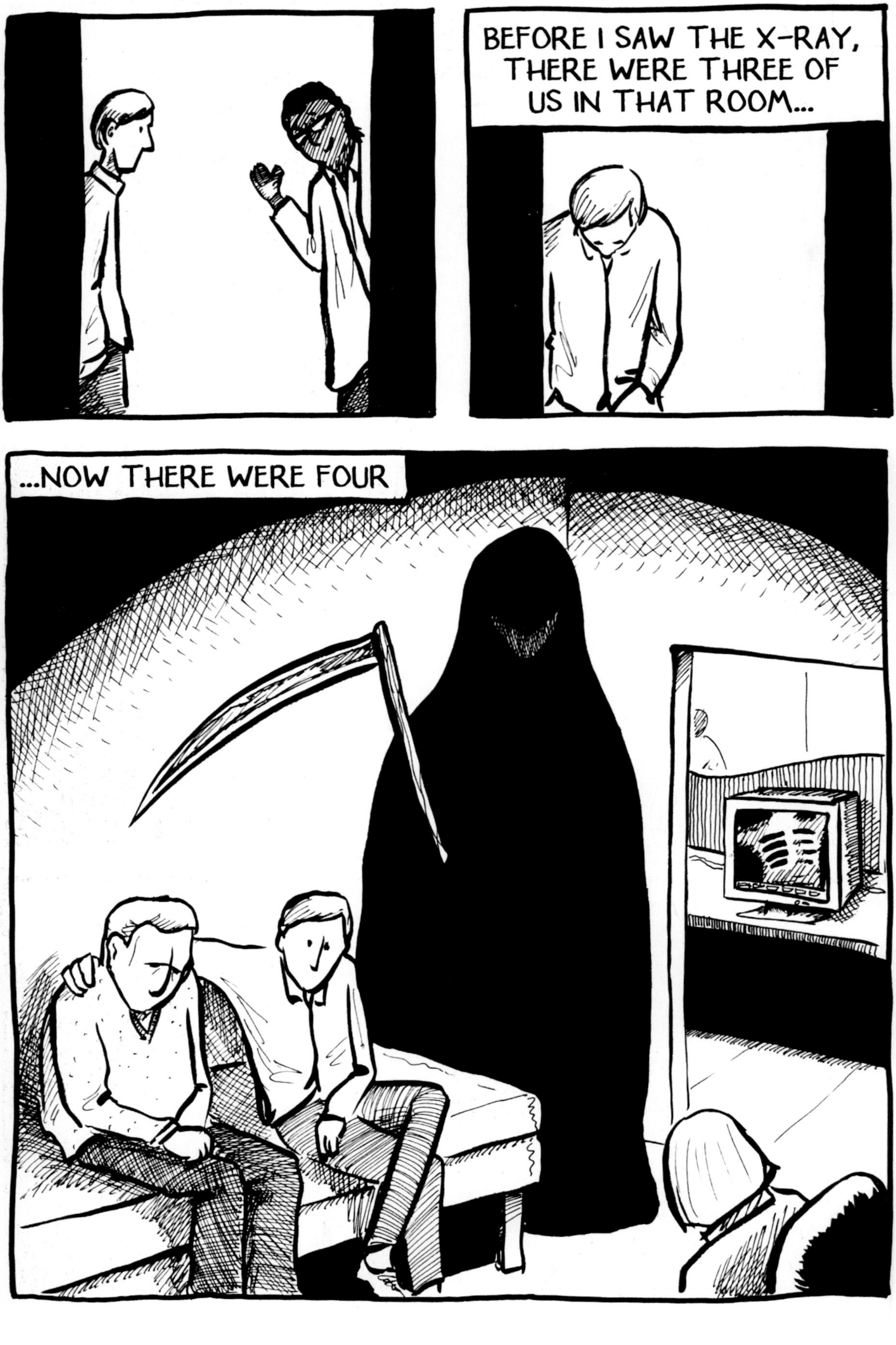
BEFORE I SAW THE X-RAY, THERE WERE THREE OF US IN THAT ROOM...
...NOW THERE WERE FOUR

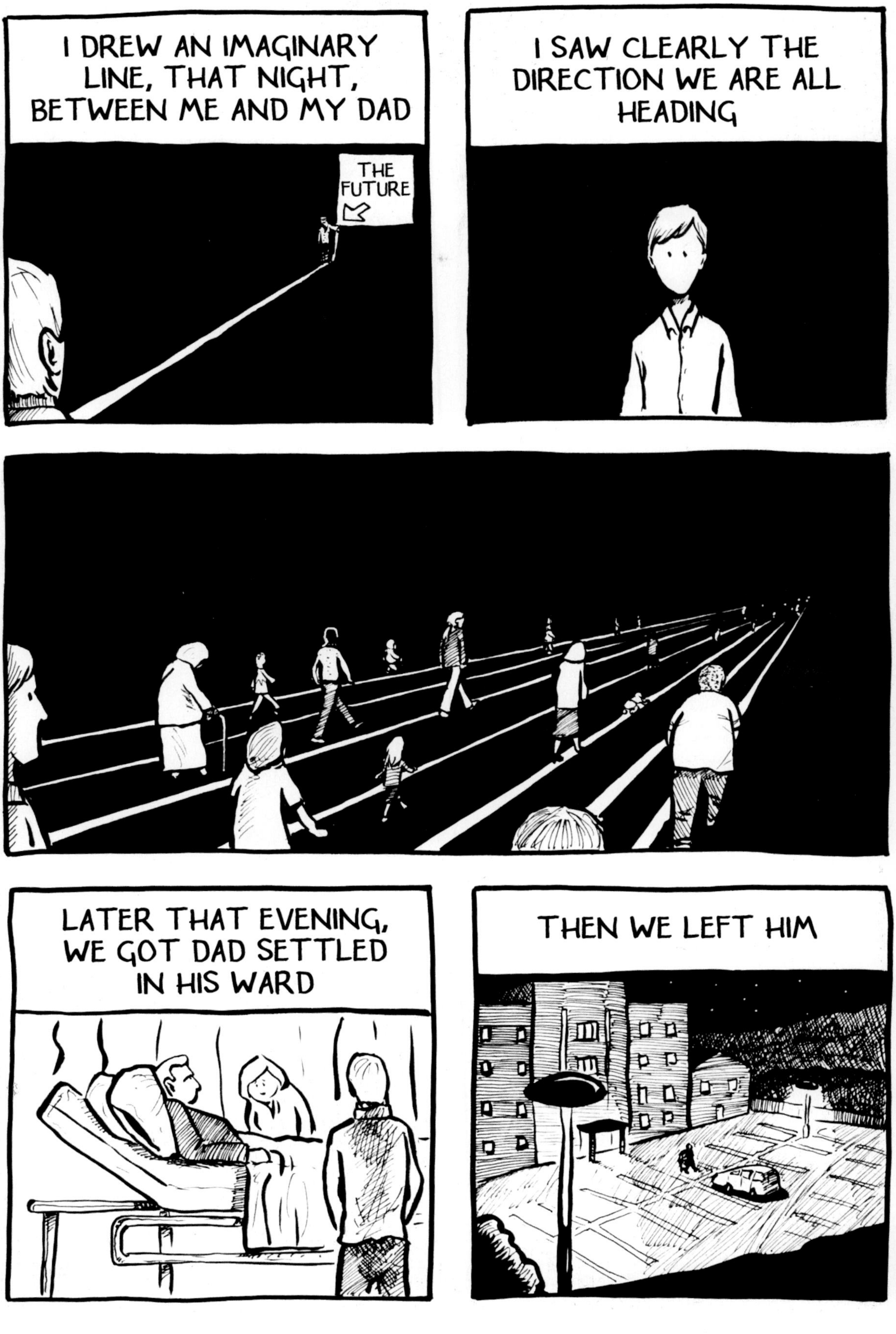
I DREW AN IMAGINARY LINE, THAT NIGHT, BETWEEN ME AND MY DAD
THE FUTURE
I SAW CLEARLY THE DIRECTION WE ARE ALL HEADING
LATER THAT EVENING, WE GOT DAD SETTLED IN HIS WARD
THEN WE LEFT HIM

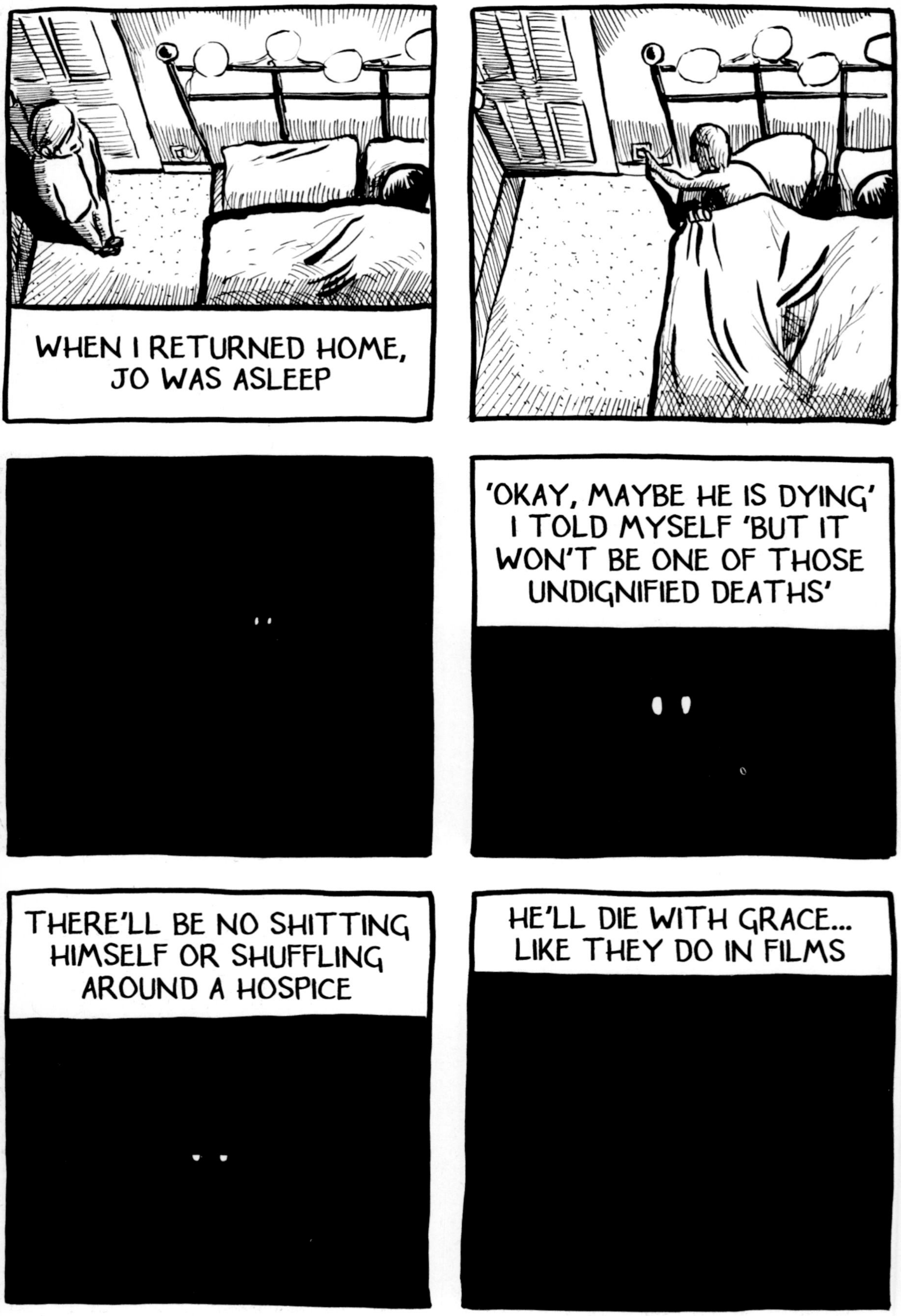
WHEN I RETURNED HOME, JO WAS ASLEEP
'OKAY, MAYBE HE IS DYING' I TOLD MYSELF 'BUT IT WON'T BE ONE OF THOSE UNDIGNIFIED DEATHS'
THERE'LL BE NO SHITTING HIMSELF OR SHUFFLING AROUND A HOSPICE
HE'LL DIE WITH GRACE... LIKE THEY DO IN FILMS

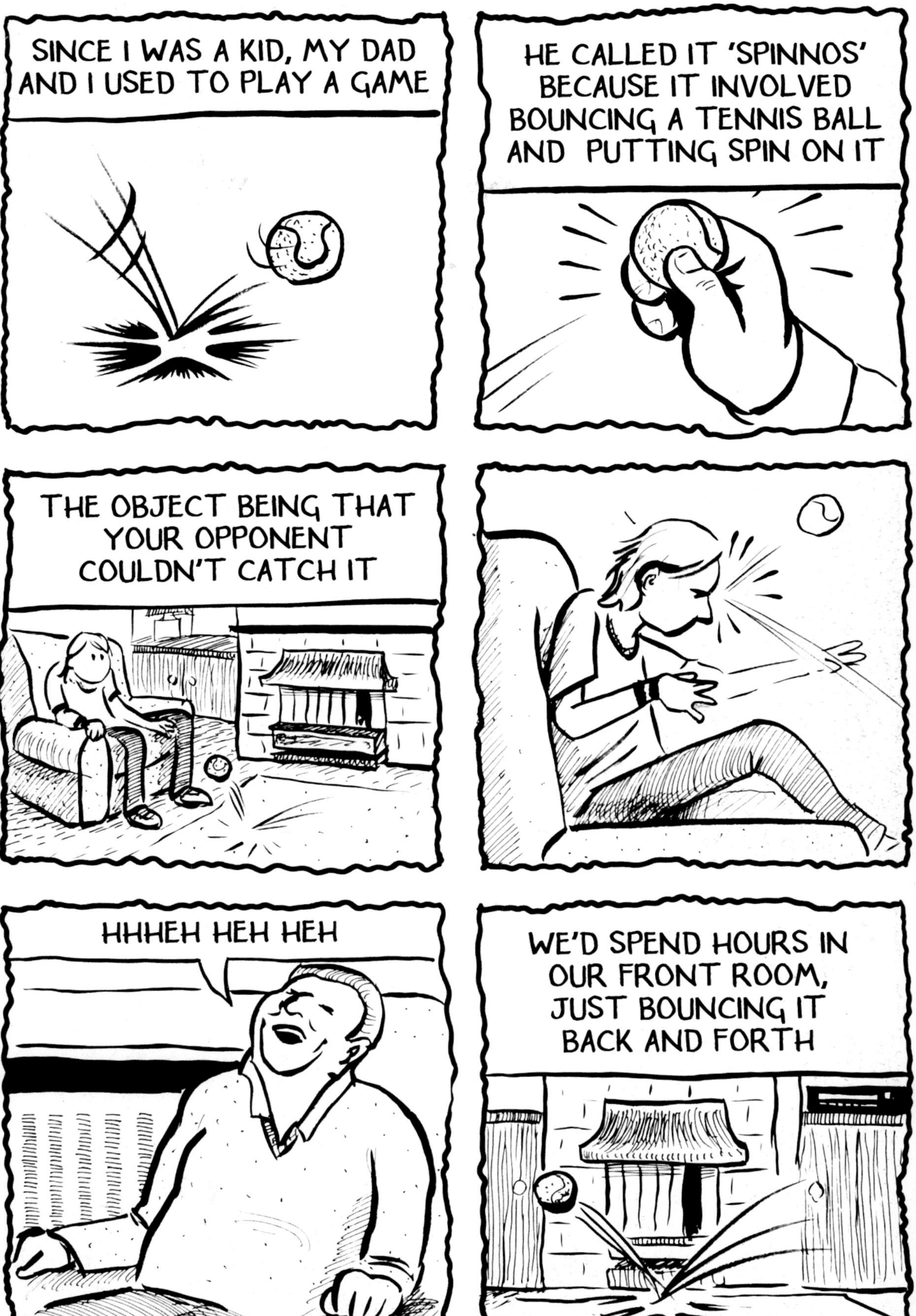
SINCE I WAS A KID, MY DAD AND I USED TO PLAY A GAME
HE CALLED IT 'SPINNOS' BECAUSE IT INVOLVED BOUNCING A TENNIS BALL AND PUTTING SPIN ON IT
THE OBJECT BEING THAT YOUR OPPONENT COULDN'T CATCH IT
HHHEH HEH HEH
WE'D SPEND HOURS IN OUR FRONT ROOM, JUST BOUNCING IT BACK AND FORTH

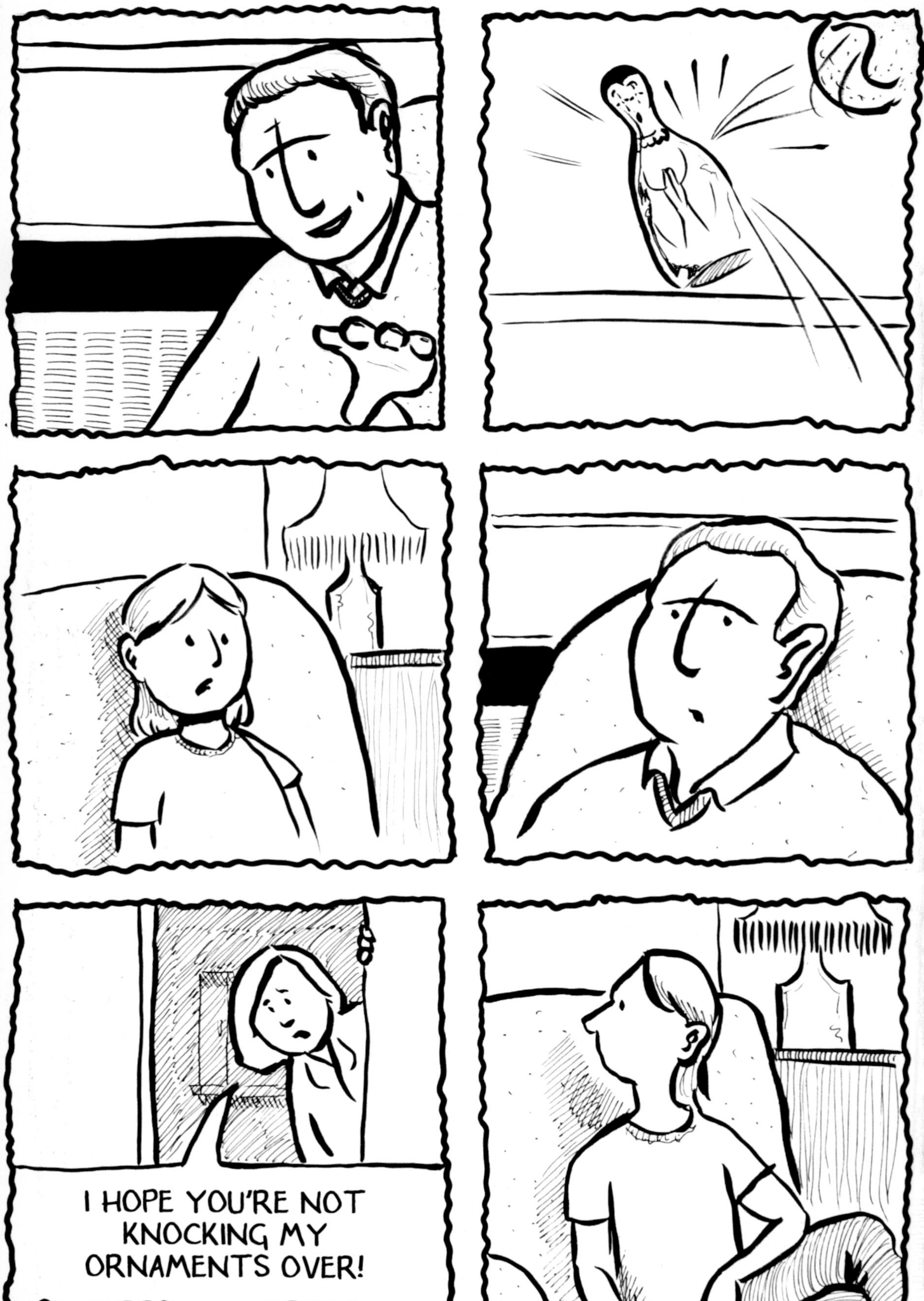
I HOPE YOU'RE NOT KNOCKING MY ORNAMENTS OVER!

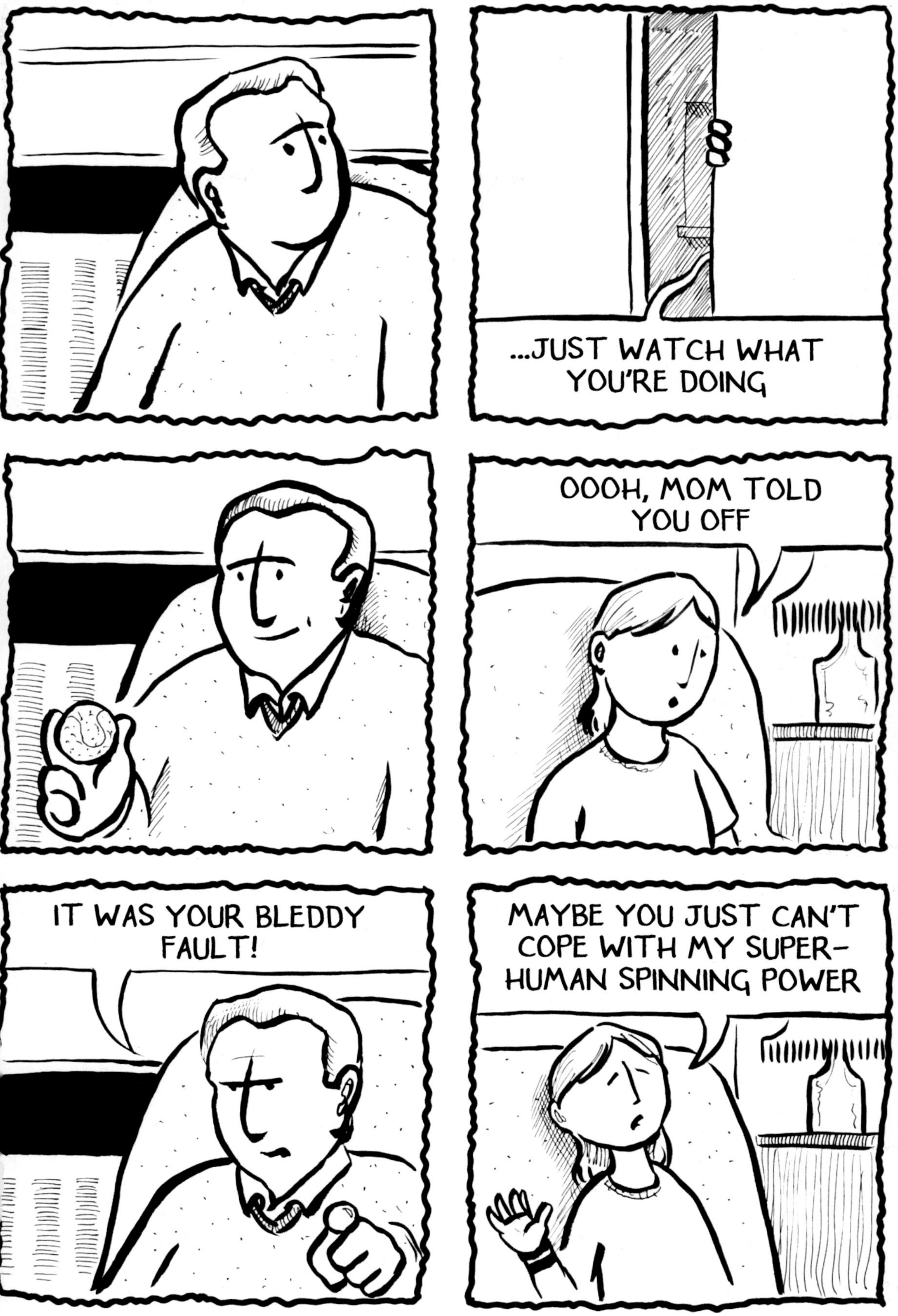
...JUST WATCH WHAT YOU'RE DOING
OOOH, MOM TOLD YOU OFF
IT WAS YOUR BLEDDY FAULT!
MAYBE YOU JUST CAN'T COPE WITH MY SUPER-HUMAN SPINNING POWER

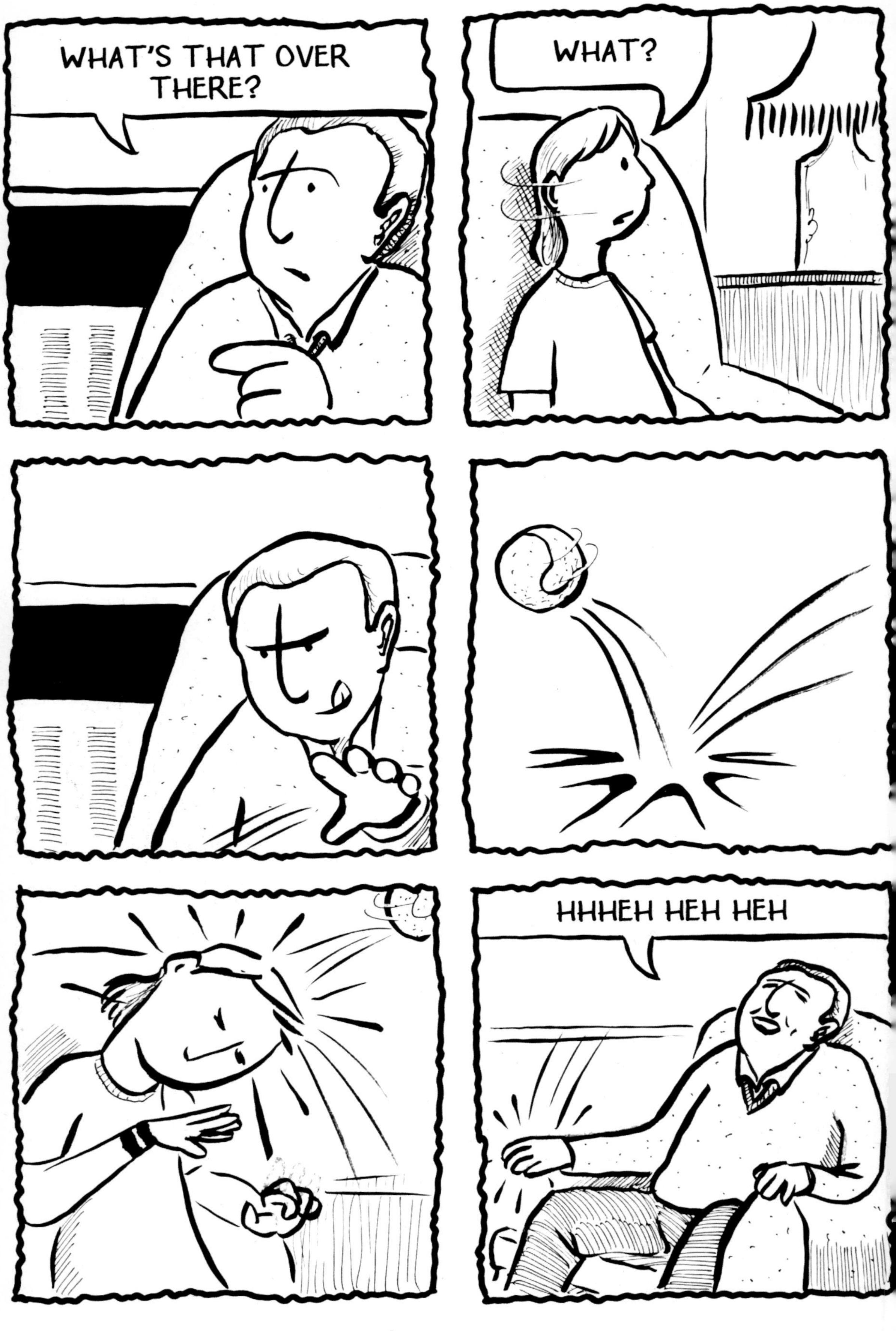
WHAT'S THAT OVER THERE?
WHAT?
HHHEH HEH HEH

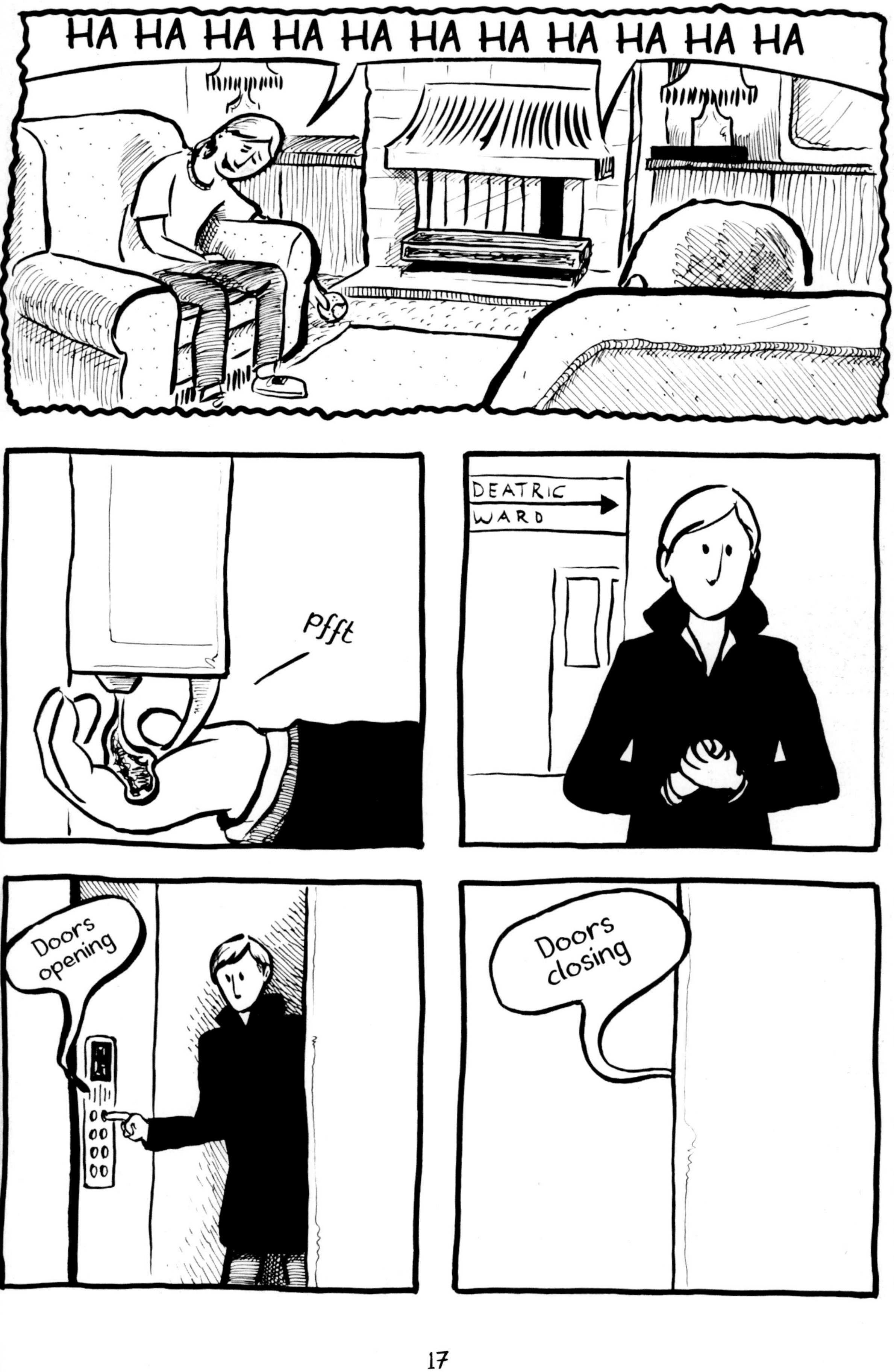
HA HA HA HA HA HA HA HA HA HA HA
pfft
DEATRIC WARD
Doors opening
Doors closing

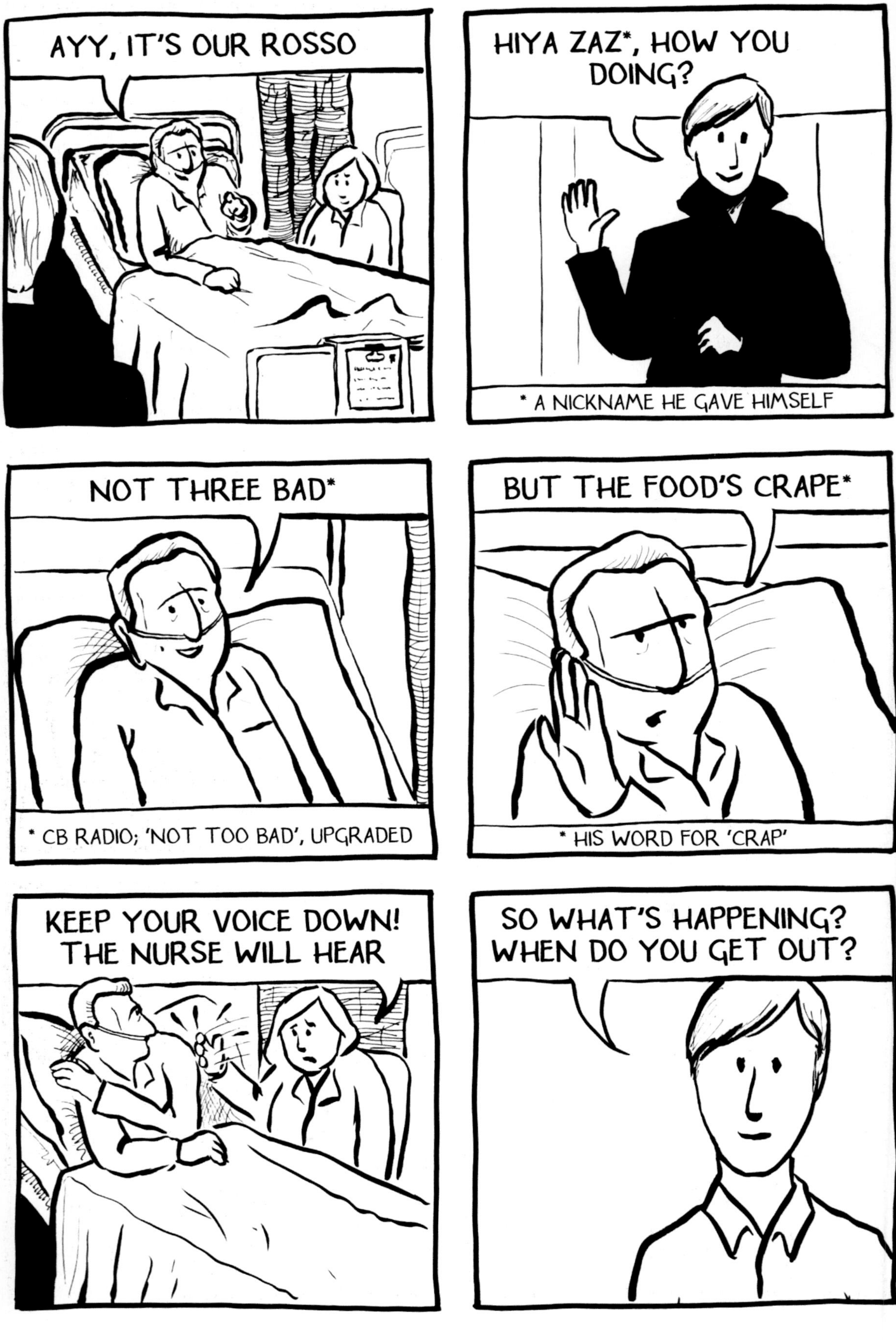
AYY, IT'S OUR ROSSO
HIYA ZAZ*, HOW YOU DOING?
* A NICKNAME HE GAVE HIMSELF
NOT THREE BAD*
* CB RADIO; 'NOT TOO BAD', UPGRADED
BUT THE FOOD'S CRAPE*
* HIS WORD FOR 'CRAP'
KEEP YOUR VOICE DOWN! THE NURSE WILL HEAR
SO WHAT'S HAPPENING? WHEN DO YOU GET OUT?

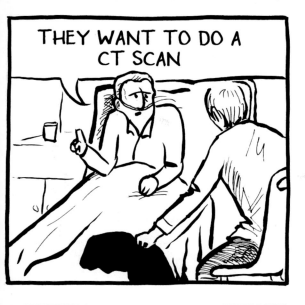
THEY WANT TO DO A CT SCAN

...BUT I'M NOT GOING IN ONE OF THOSE AGAIN

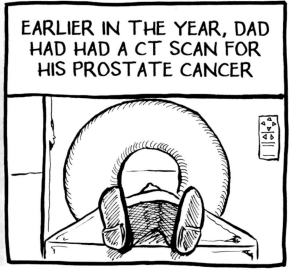
EARLIER IN THE YEAR, DAD HAD HAD A CT SCAN FOR HIS PROSTATE CANCER

...BUT WAS OVERCOME BY A NEW FOUND CLAUSTROPHOBIA

GET ME OUT!

THEY CAN FORGET IT

BUT JOHN, THEY NEED TO FIND OUT WHAT'S WRONG WITH YOU!

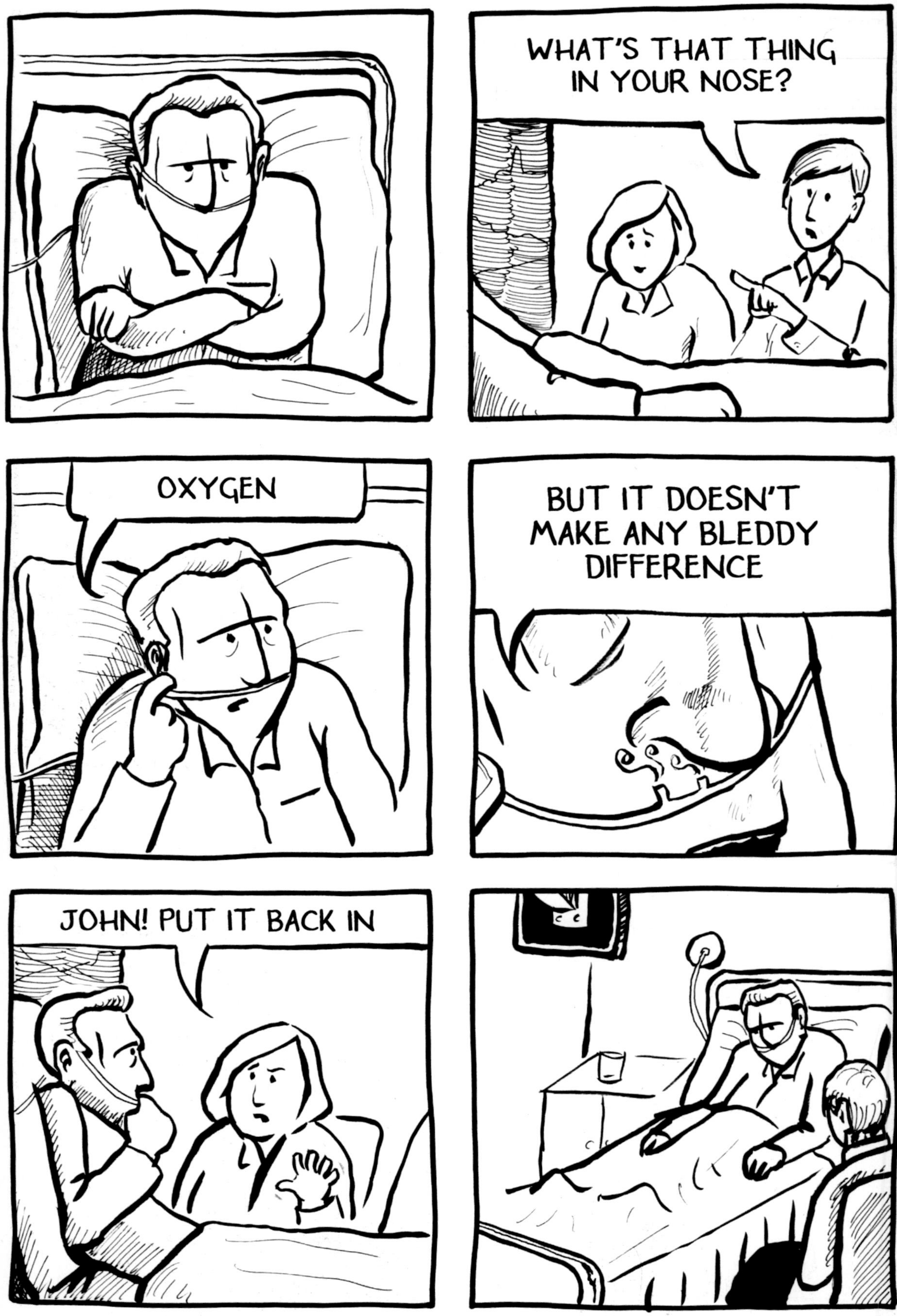
WHAT'S THAT THING IN YOUR NOSE?
OXYGEN
BUT IT DOESN'T MAKE ANY BLEDDY DIFFERENCE
JOHN! PUT IT BACK IN

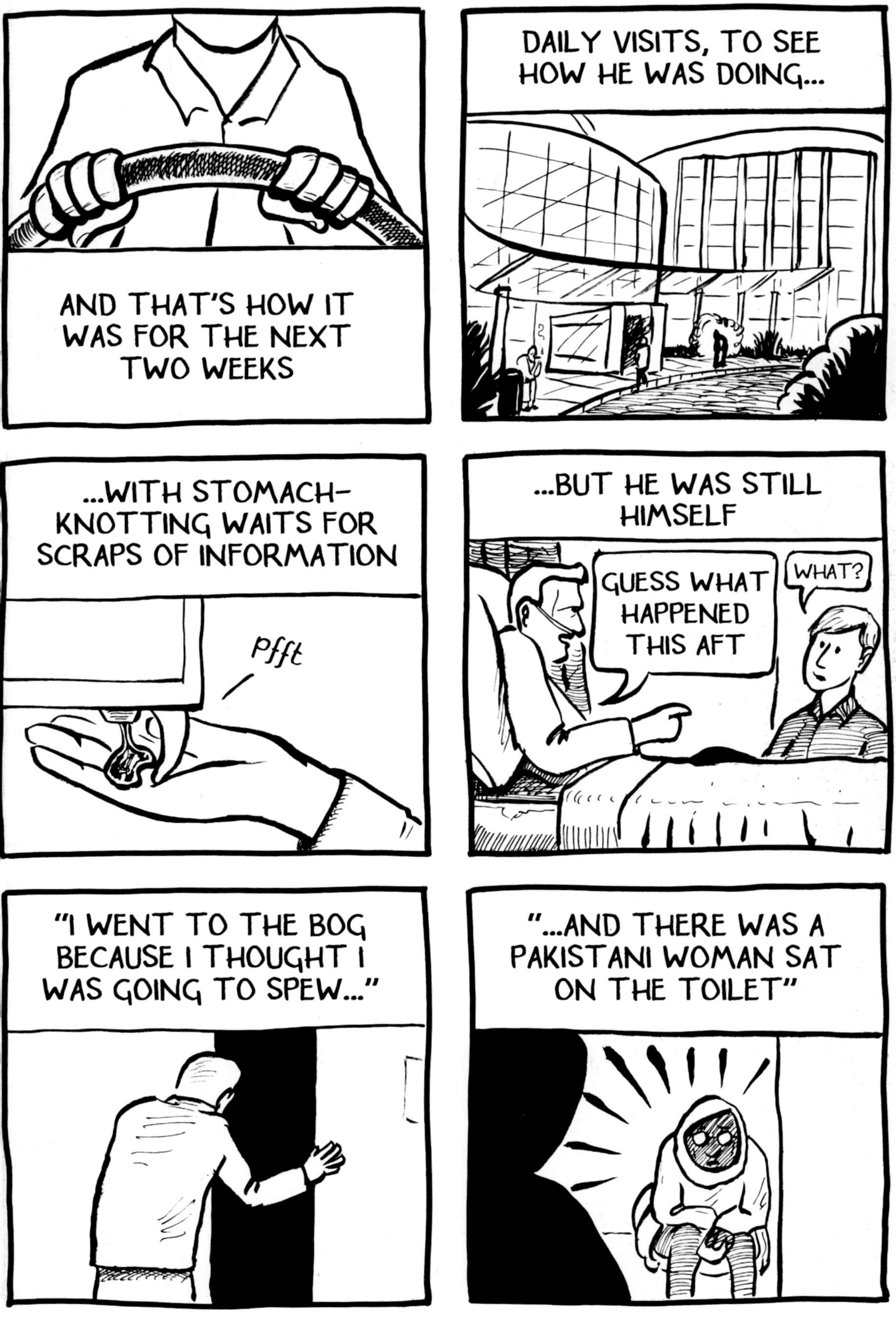
AND THAT'S HOW IT WAS FOR THE NEXT TWO WEEKS
DAILY VISITS, TO SEE HOW HE WAS DOING...
...WITH STOMACH-KNOTTING WAITS FOR SCRAPS OF INFORMATION
Pfft
...BUT HE WAS STILL HIMSELF
GUESS WHAT HAPPENED THIS AFT
WHAT?
"I WENT TO THE BOG BECAUSE I THOUGHT I WAS GOING TO SPEW..."
"...AND THERE WAS A PAKISTANI WOMAN SAT ON THE TOILET"

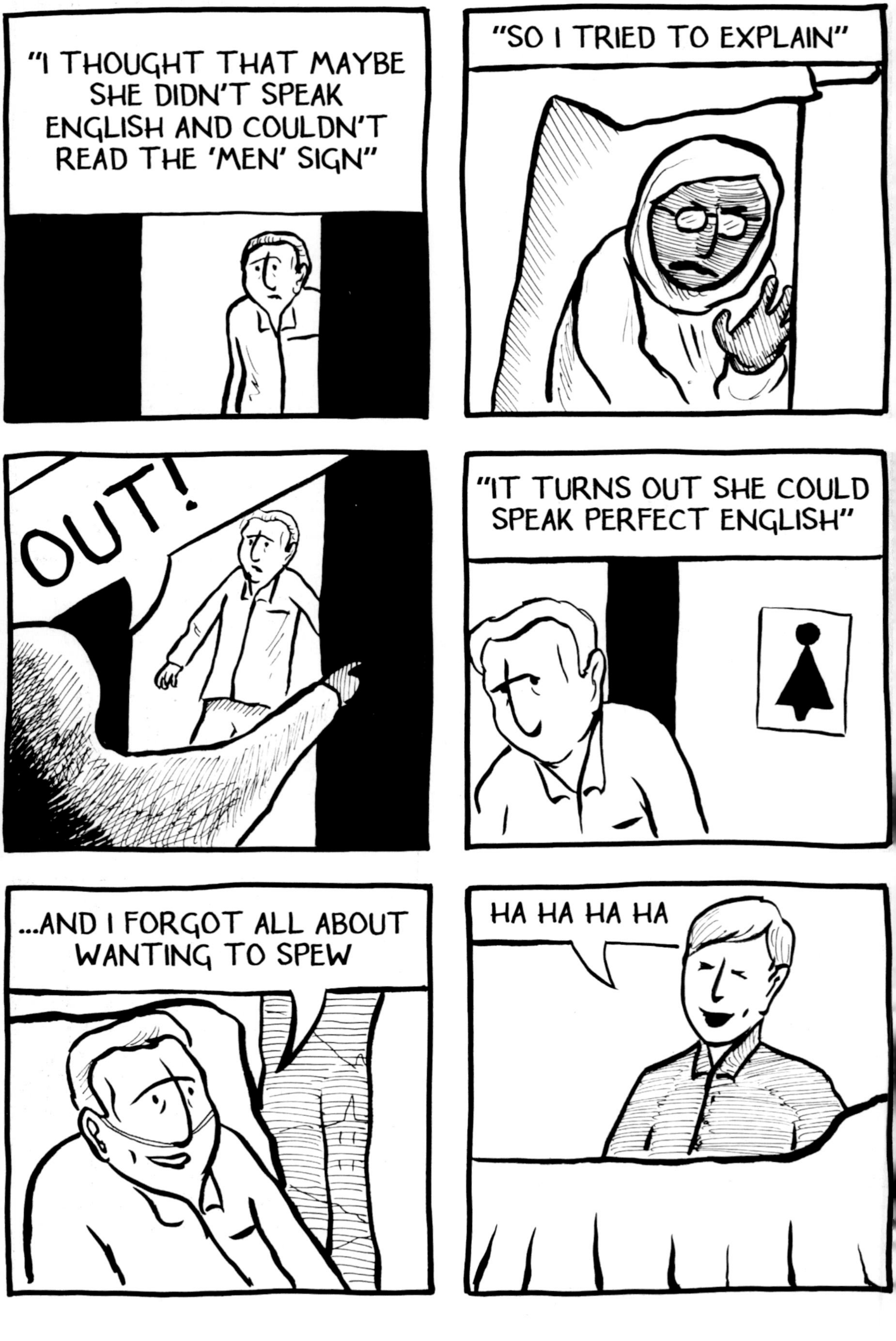

"I THOUGHT THAT MAYBE SHE DIDN'T SPEAK ENGLISH AND COULDN'T READ THE 'MEN' SIGN"
"SO I TRIED TO EXPLAIN"
OUT!
"IT TURNS OUT SHE COULD SPEAK PERFECT ENGLISH"
...AND I FORGOT ALL ABOUT WANTING TO SPEW
HA HA HA HA

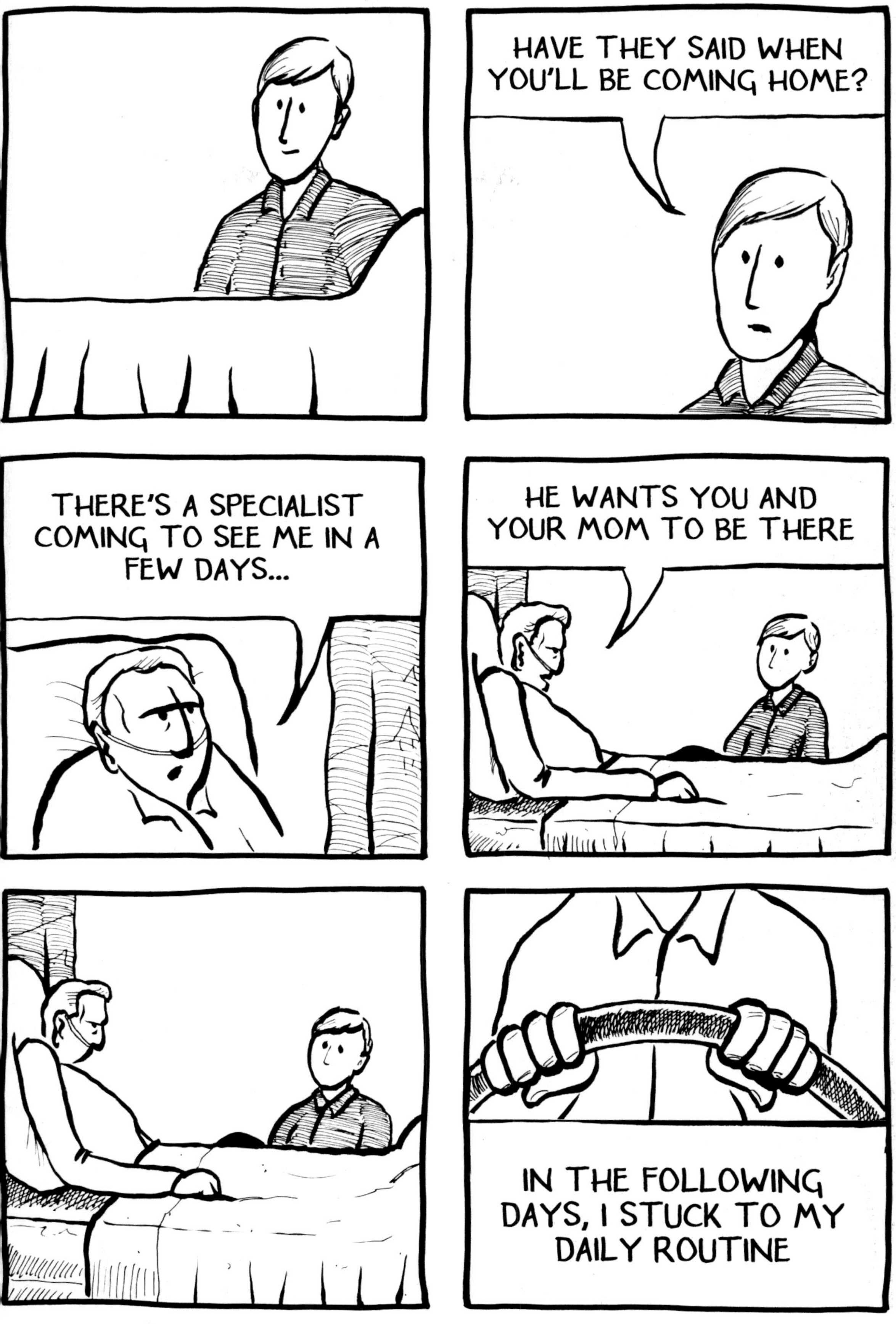
HAVE THEY SAID WHEN YOU'LL BE COMING HOME?
THERE'S A SPECIALIST COMING TO SEE ME IN A FEW DAYS...
HE WANTS YOU AND YOUR MOM TO BE THERE
IN THE FOLLOWING DAYS, I STUCK TO MY DAILY ROUTINE

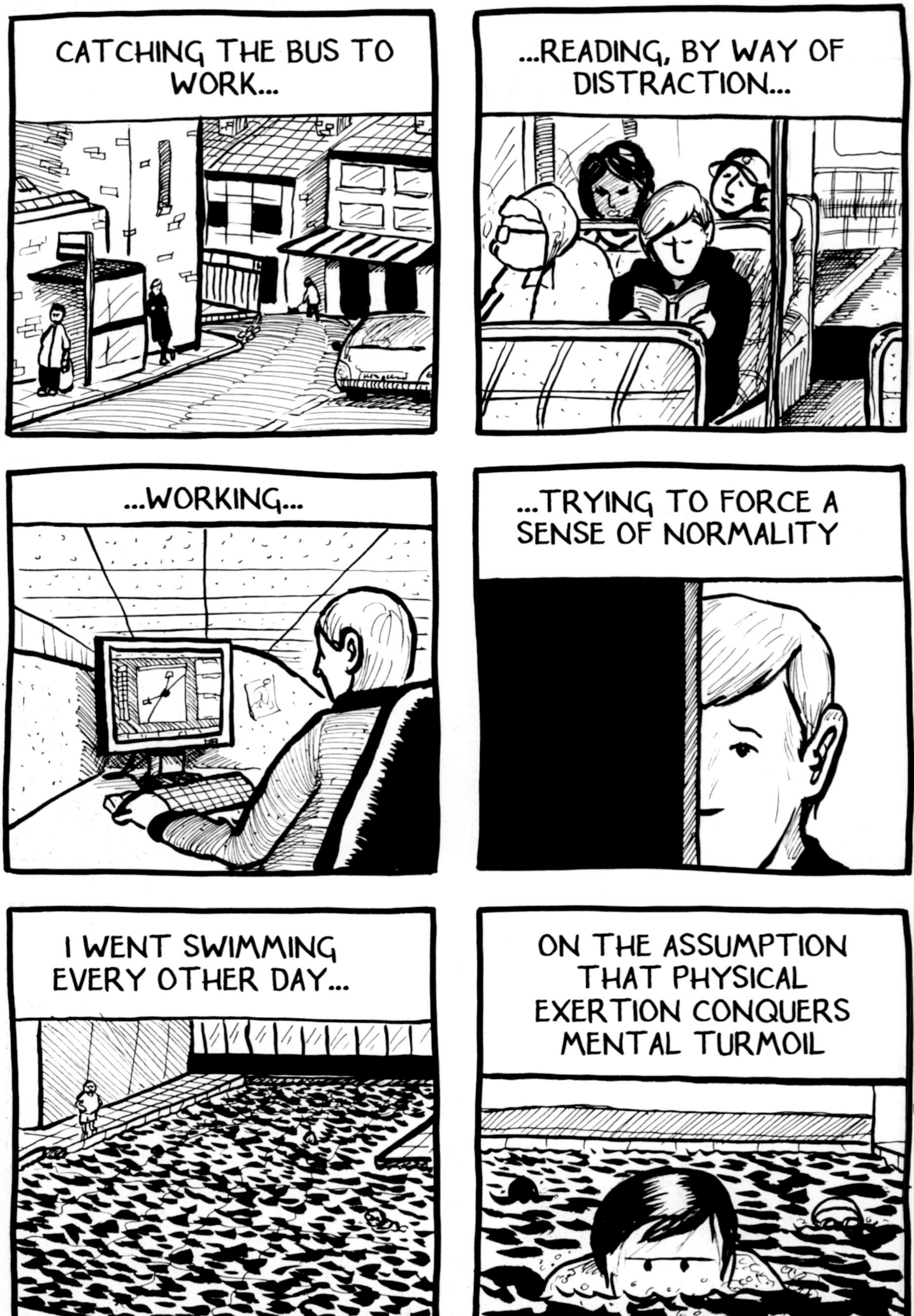
CATCHING THE BUS TO WORK...
...READING, BY WAY OF DISTRACTION...
...WORKING...
...TRYING TO FORCE A SENSE OF NORMALITY
I WENT SWIMMING EVERY OTHER DAY...
ON THE ASSUMPTION THAT PHYSICAL EXERTION CONQUERS MENTAL TURMOIL

I'D MEET MY FRIEND MARTIN, WITH WHOM I COULD NOT ONLY CONFIDE...

...BUT ALSO RELY UPON FOR PHILOSOPHICAL OFFERINGS

SOMETHING'S GOT TO GET YOU IN THE END

THE PROSPECT OF DEATH IS SUPPOSED TO GALVANISE US INTO ATTENDING TO YOUR OWN MORTALITY...

HAVING KIDS, MAKING ART, INVADING OTHER COUNTRIES...I'M TOO LAZY FOR ANY OF THAT

I JUST STARE INTO THE ABYSS IN ABJECT HORROR

DOESN'T EVERYONE?

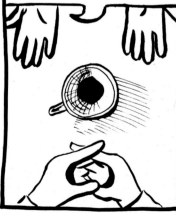

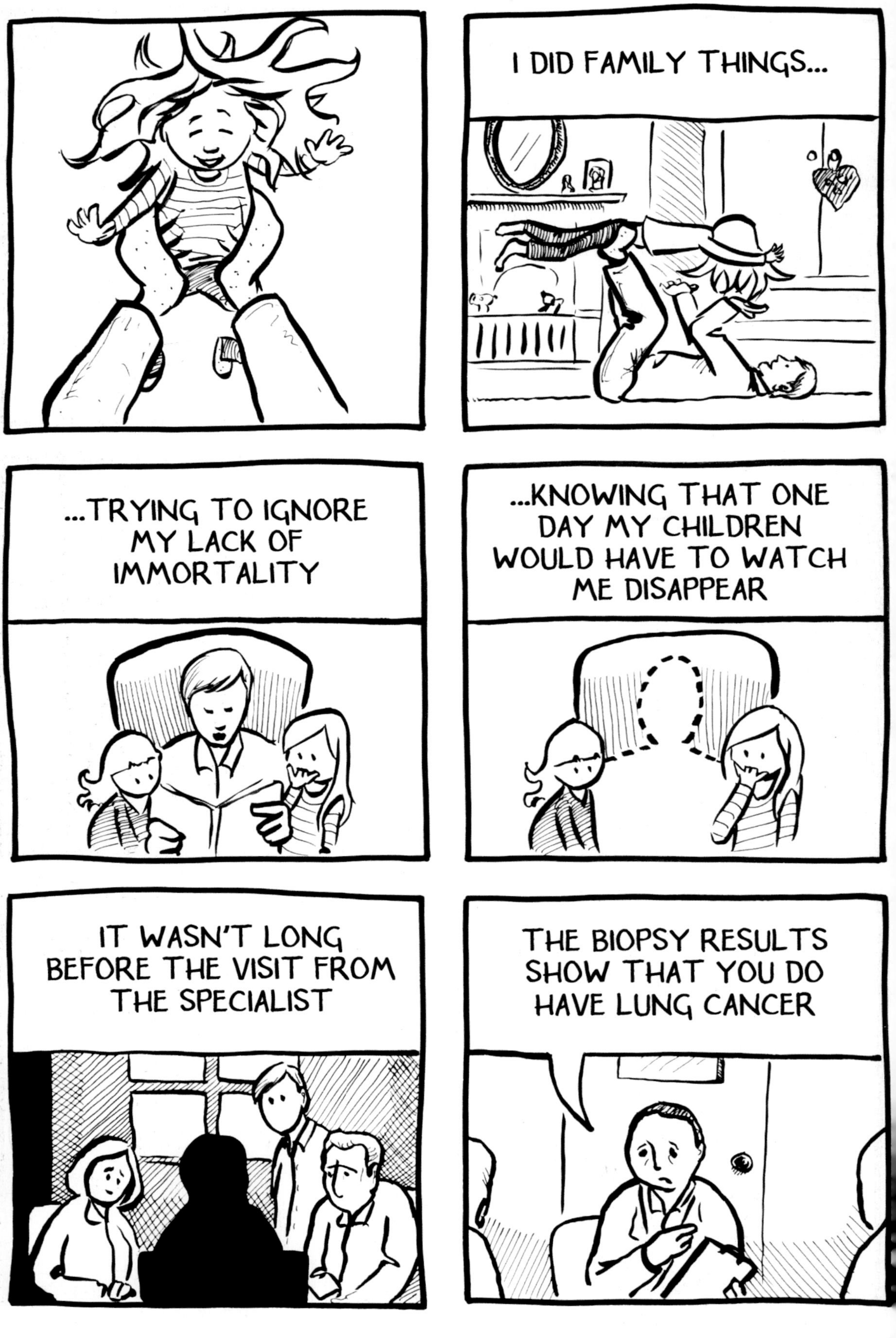
I DID FAMILY THINGS...
...TRYING TO IGNORE MY LACK OF IMMORTALITY
...KNOWING THAT ONE DAY MY CHILDREN WOULD HAVE TO WATCH ME DISAPPEAR
IT WASN'T LONG BEFORE THE VISIT FROM THE SPECIALIST
THE BIOPSY RESULTS SHOW THAT YOU DO HAVE LUNG CANCER

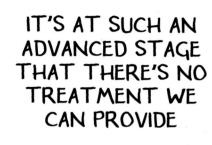

IT'S SPREAD ACROSS BOTH LUNGS AND THE WINDPIPE

IT'S AT SUCH AN ADVANCED STAGE THAT THERE'S NO TREATMENT WE CAN PROVIDE

Sorry

CAN I GO HOME NOW?

MOM AND I LEFT THE HOSPITAL. THEY RELEASED DAD A DAY LATER

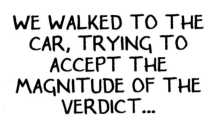

WE WALKED TO THE CAR, TRYING TO ACCEPT THE MAGNITUDE OF THE VERDICT...

...WITHOUT SUCCESS

WHAT AM I GOING TO DO? HE'S BEEN PART OF MY LIFE SINCE I WAS 16

I KNOW ABOUT GENE PROPOGATION; THAT OUR BODIES ARE JUST ENABLERS

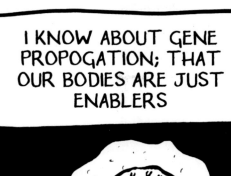

CONTAINERS, TO PRESERVE OUR GENES FOR THE NEXT GENERATION

WE SPEND OUR LIVES PROTECTING OUR BODIES AND REPRODUCING, TO KEEP THE THREAD OF GENES CONTINUOUS

AS SOON AS WE ARE CERTAIN THAT OUR OFFSPRING CAN PROSPER, WE BECOME DISPOSABLE

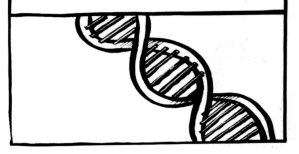

A SPECIES THAT CARES ABOUT IT'S OFFSPRING WILL FLOURISH

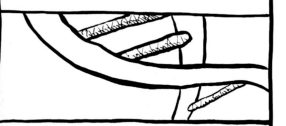

AND THERE IS THE IRONY:

THOSE WHO LOVE WILL BE REWARDED WITH THE ENDLESS CYCLE OF BIRTH AND DEATH

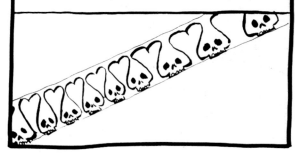

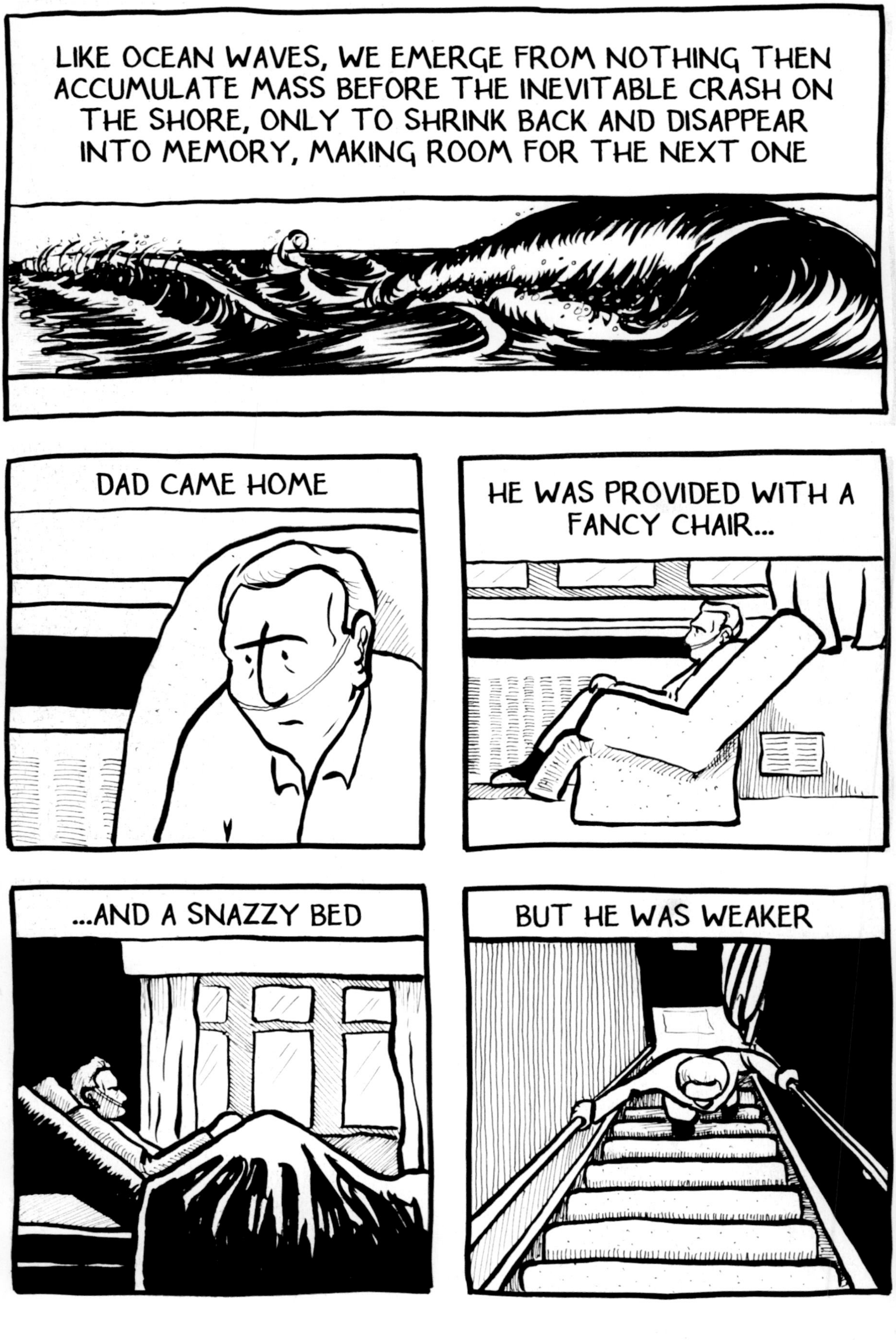
LIKE OCEAN WAVES, WE EMERGE FROM NOTHING THEN ACCUMULATE MASS BEFORE THE INEVITABLE CRASH ON THE SHORE, ONLY TO SHRINK BACK AND DISAPPEAR INTO MEMORY, MAKING ROOM FOR THE NEXT ONE
DAD CAME HOME
HE WAS PROVIDED WITH A FANCY CHAIR...
...AND A SNAZZY BED
BUT HE WAS WEAKER

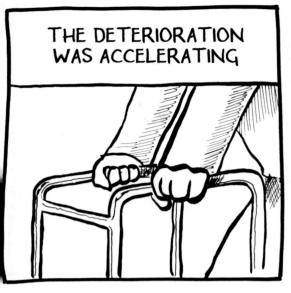

THE DETERIORATION WAS ACCELERATING

THEN ONE NIGHT...

bzz bzz

WHAT'S UP MOM?

YES, I'M IN BED BUT IT'S OK TO TALK

WHAT'S WRONG?

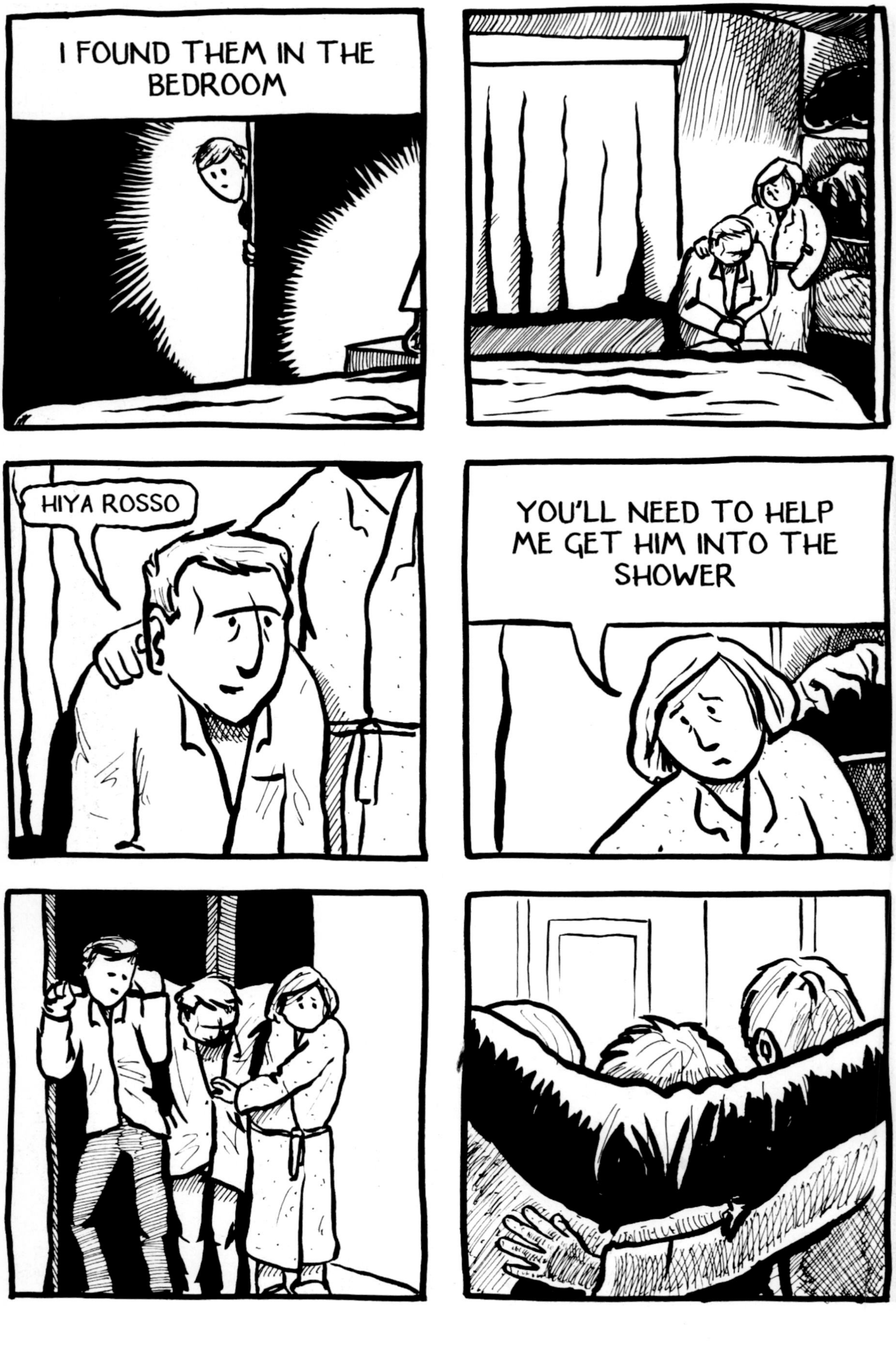
I FOUND THEM IN THE BEDROOM
HIYA ROSSO
YOU'LL NEED TO HELP ME GET HIM INTO THE SHOWER

I'LL GET SOME TOWELS

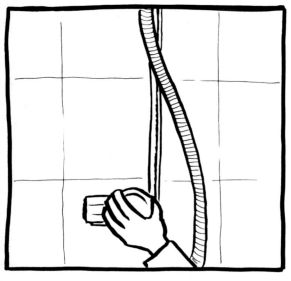

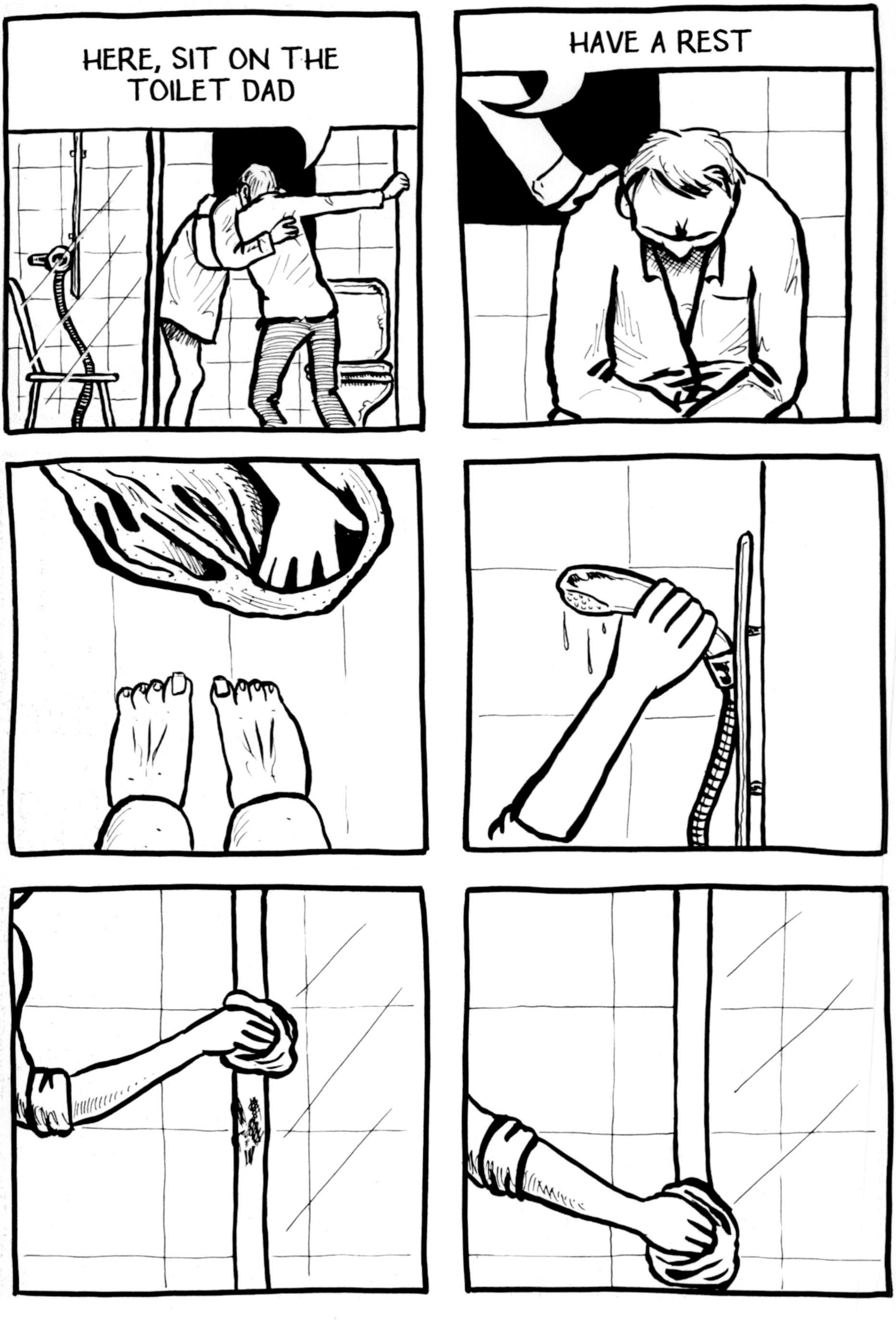
HERE, SIT ON THE TOILET DAD
HAVE A REST

I'LL PUT THESE TOWELS IN THE WASH

I'VE BROUGHT YOUR WALKING FRAME DAD, BUT THERE'S NO RUSH

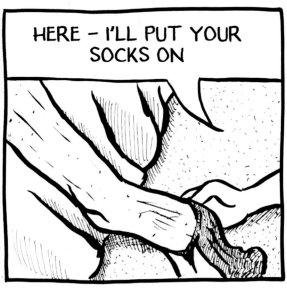

HERE – I'LL PUT YOUR SOCKS ON

HERE'S YOUR DRESSING GOWN...

...AND I'VE GOT YOU SOME CLEAN PYJAMA BOTTOMS

FUNNY, THAT

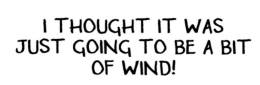

I THOUGHT IT WAS JUST GOING TO BE A BIT OF WIND!

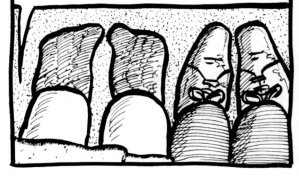

THANKS FOR COMING. YOU SHOULD GET BACK TO BED NOW

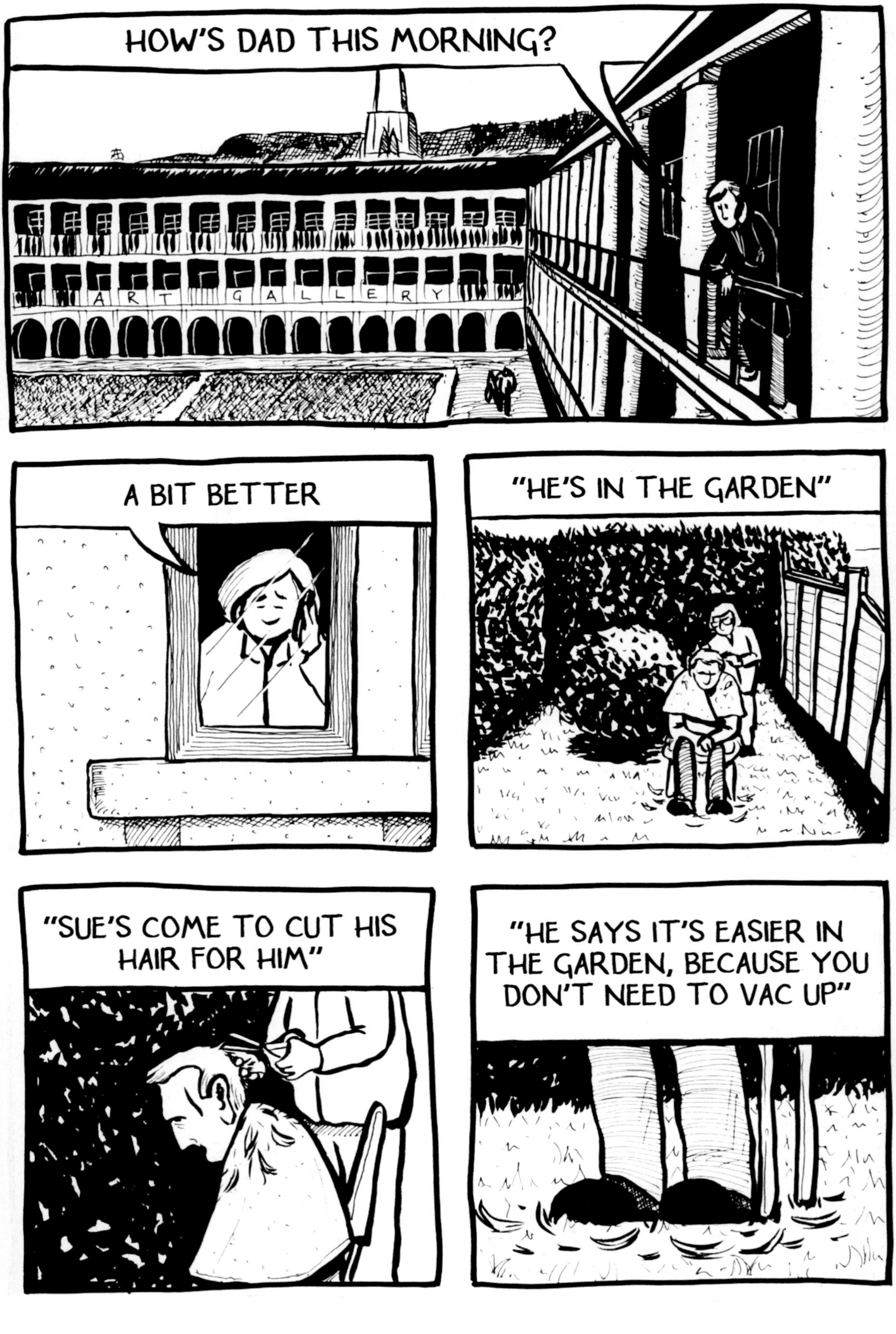
HOW'S DAD THIS MORNING?
ART GALLERY
A BIT BETTER
"HE'S IN THE GARDEN"
"SUE'S COME TO CUT HIS HAIR FOR HIM"
"HE SAYS IT'S EASIER IN THE GARDEN, BECAUSE YOU DON'T NEED TO VAC UP"

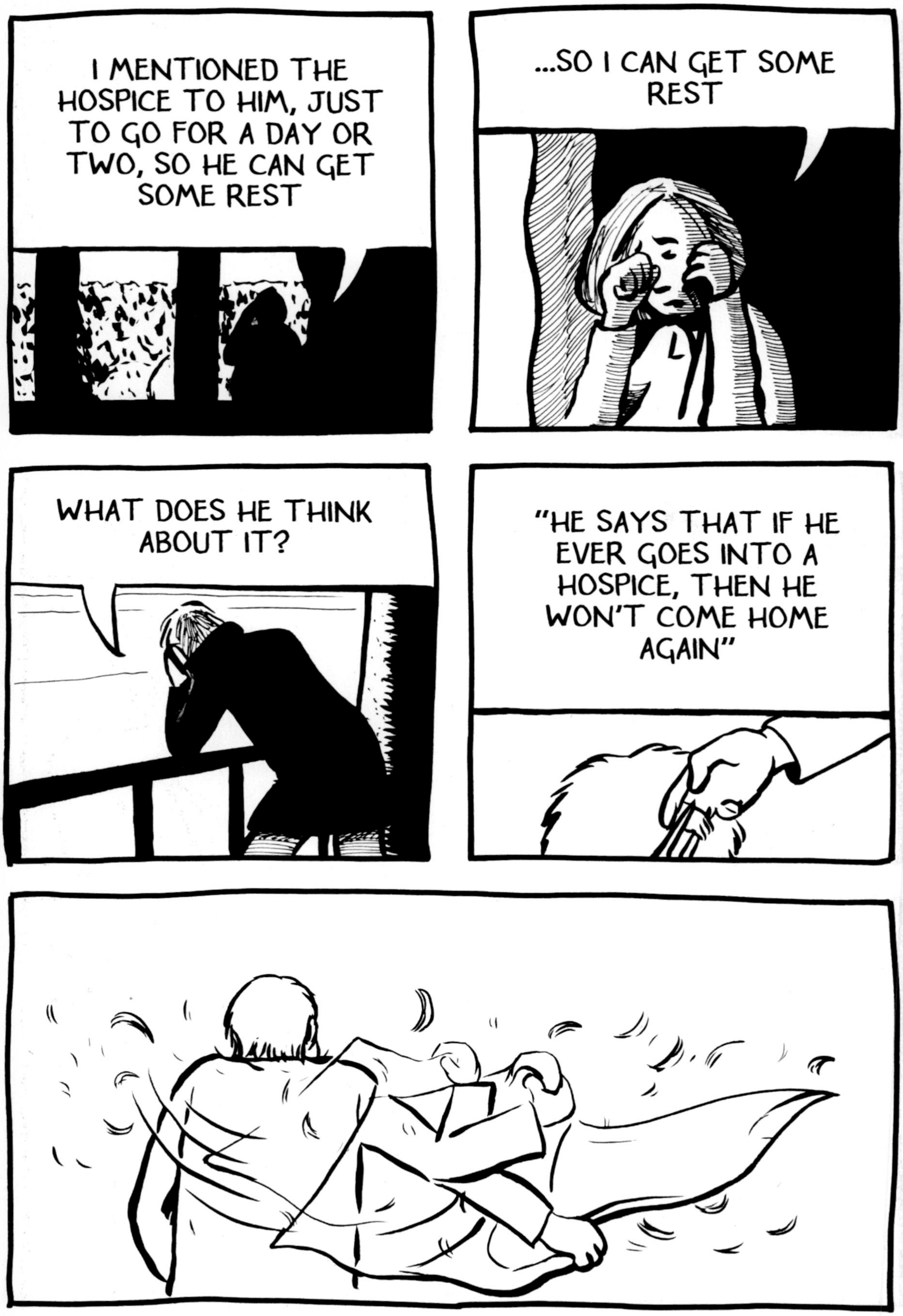
I MENTIONED THE HOSPICE TO HIM, JUST TO GO FOR A DAY OR TWO, SO HE CAN GET SOME REST
...SO I CAN GET SOME REST
WHAT DOES HE THINK ABOUT IT?
"HE SAYS THAT IF HE EVER GOES INTO A HOSPICE, THEN HE WON'T COME HOME AGAIN"

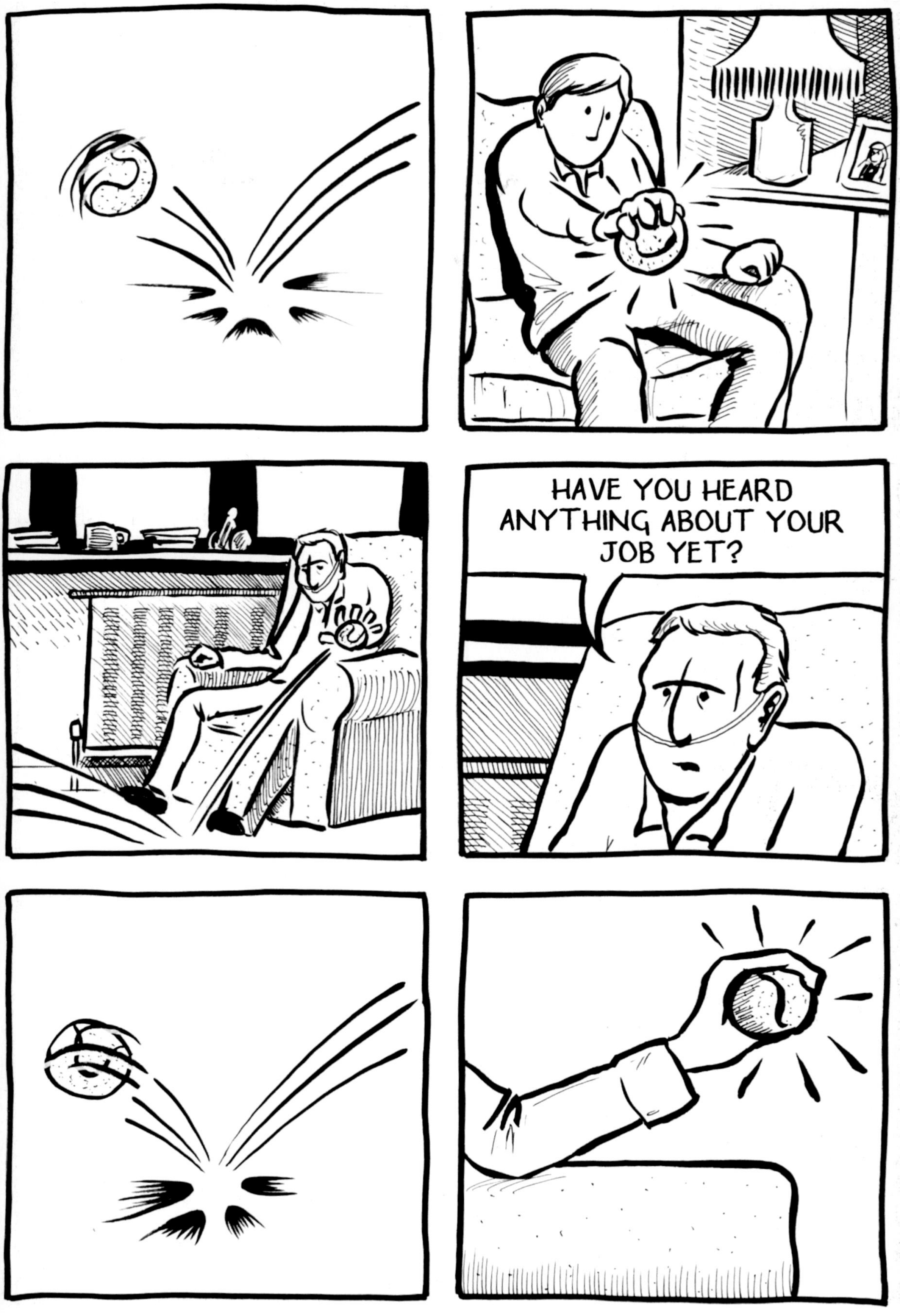
HAVE YOU HEARD ANYTHING ABOUT YOUR JOB YET?

NOT YET. I FIND OUT IN A FEW WEEKS

THE RECESSION HAD CAST DOUBT OVER THE FUTURE OF MY JOB

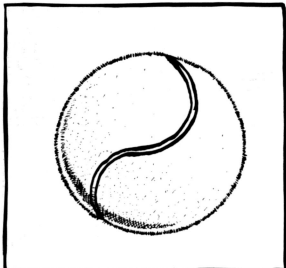

FINGERS CROSSED, EH?

MY DAD VALUED REGULAR INCOME MORE THAN ANY OTHER CAREER ASPIRATIONS

IT WAS IMPORTANT TO HIM THAT I WAS 'KEPT ON'

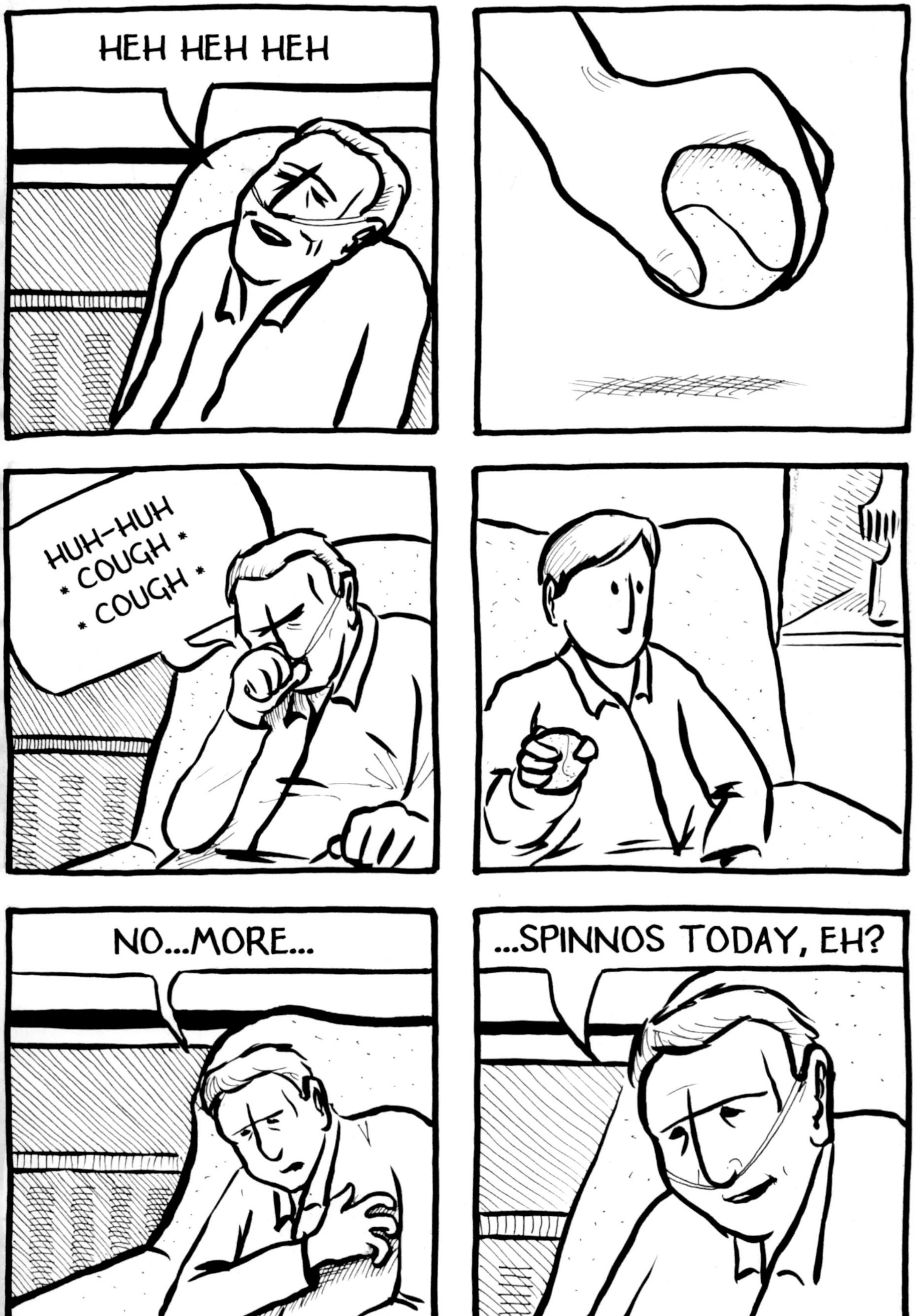
HEH HEH HEH
HUH-HUH * COUGH * * COUGH *
NO...MORE...
...SPINNOS TODAY, EH?

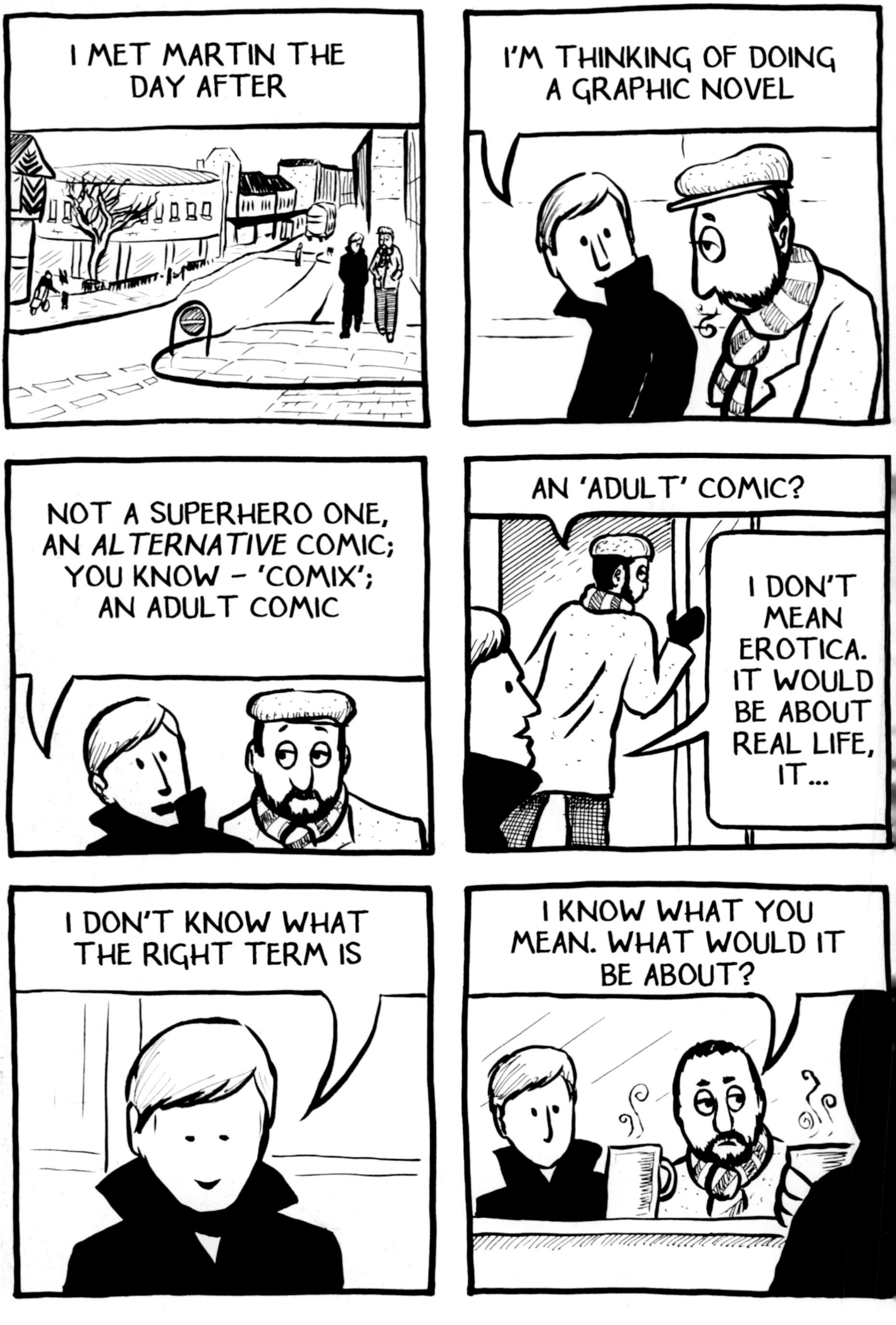
I MET MARTIN THE DAY AFTER
I'M THINKING OF DOING A GRAPHIC NOVEL
NOT A SUPERHERO ONE, AN *ALTERNATIVE* COMIC; YOU KNOW – 'COMIX'; AN ADULT COMIC
AN 'ADULT' COMIC?
I DON'T MEAN EROTICA. IT WOULD BE ABOUT REAL LIFE, IT...
I DON'T KNOW WHAT THE RIGHT TERM IS
I KNOW WHAT YOU MEAN. WHAT WOULD IT BE ABOUT?

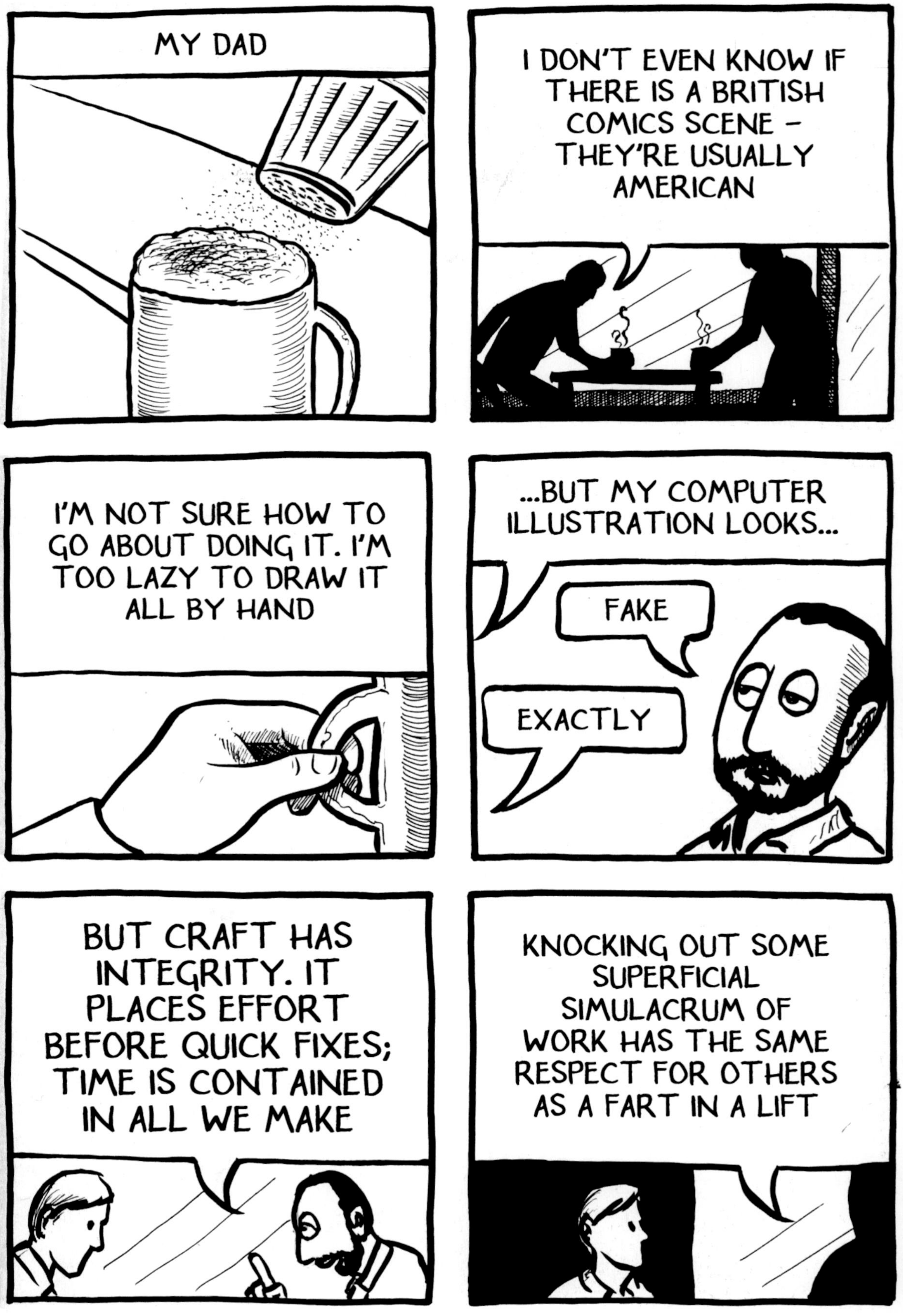
MY DAD
I DON'T EVEN KNOW IF THERE IS A BRITISH COMICS SCENE – THEY'RE USUALLY AMERICAN
I'M NOT SURE HOW TO GO ABOUT DOING IT. I'M TOO LAZY TO DRAW IT ALL BY HAND
...BUT MY COMPUTER ILLUSTRATION LOOKS...
FAKE
EXACTLY
BUT CRAFT HAS INTEGRITY. IT PLACES EFFORT BEFORE QUICK FIXES; TIME IS CONTAINED IN ALL WE MAKE
KNOCKING OUT SOME SUPERFICIAL SIMULACRUM OF WORK HAS THE SAME RESPECT FOR OTHERS AS A FART IN A LIFT

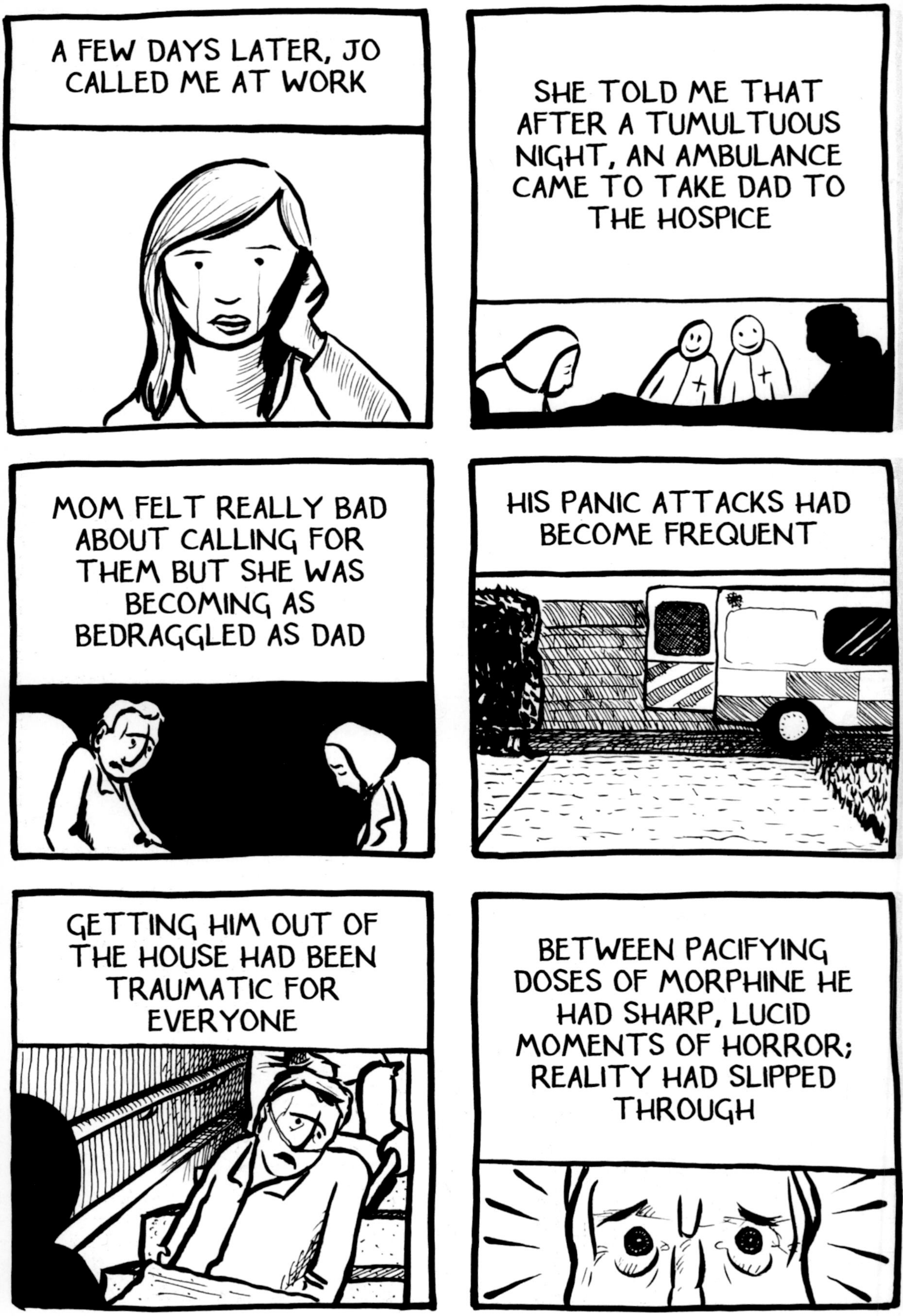
A FEW DAYS LATER, JO CALLED ME AT WORK
SHE TOLD ME THAT AFTER A TUMULTUOUS NIGHT, AN AMBULANCE CAME TO TAKE DAD TO THE HOSPICE
MOM FELT REALLY BAD ABOUT CALLING FOR THEM BUT SHE WAS BECOMING AS BEDRAGGLED AS DAD
HIS PANIC ATTACKS HAD BECOME FREQUENT
GETTING HIM OUT OF THE HOUSE HAD BEEN TRAUMATIC FOR EVERYONE
BETWEEN PACIFYING DOSES OF MORPHINE HE HAD SHARP, LUCID MOMENTS OF HORROR; REALITY HAD SLIPPED THROUGH

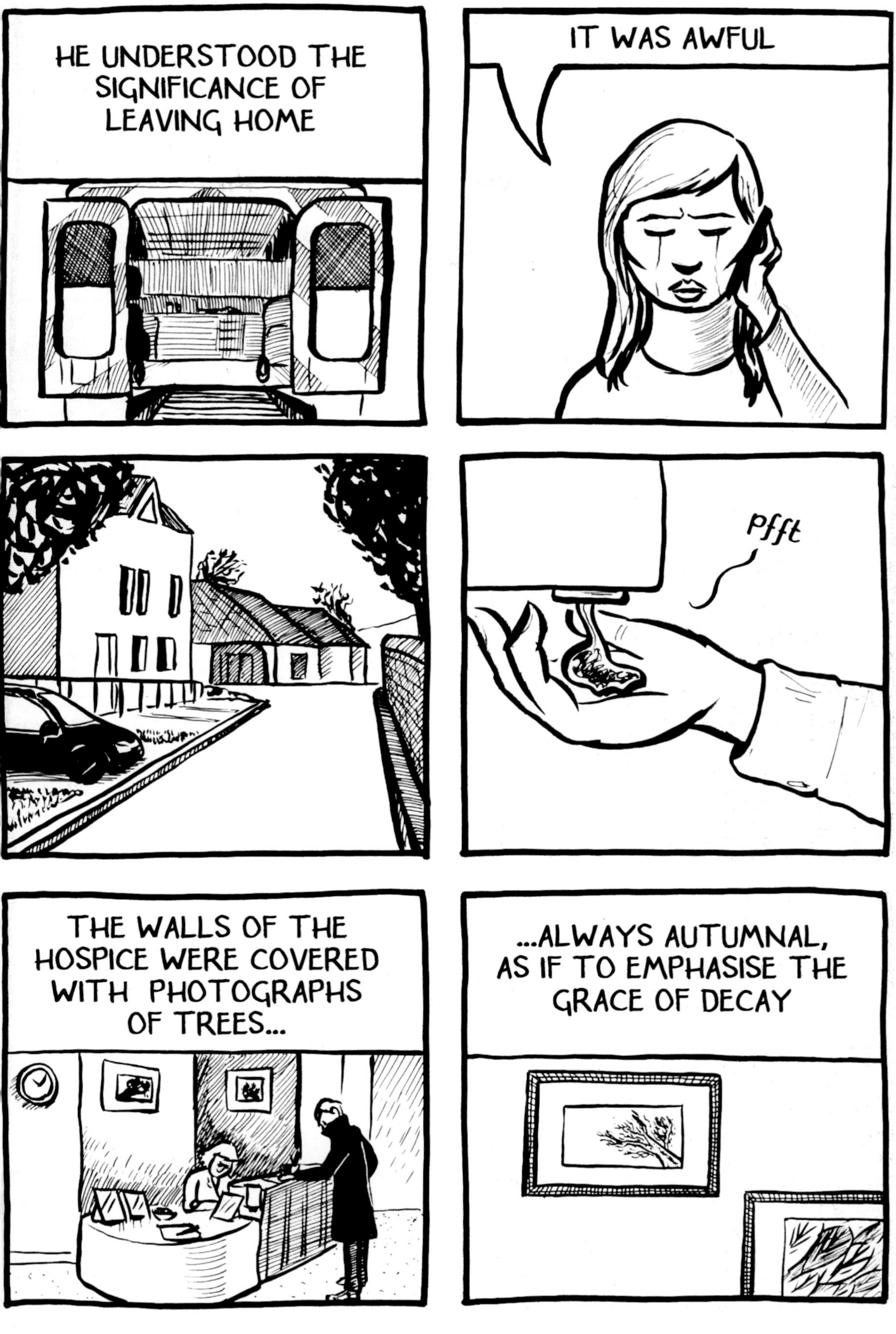
HE UNDERSTOOD THE SIGNIFICANCE OF LEAVING HOME
IT WAS AWFUL
Pfft
THE WALLS OF THE HOSPICE WERE COVERED WITH PHOTOGRAPHS OF TREES...
...ALWAYS AUTUMNAL, AS IF TO EMPHASISE THE GRACE OF DECAY

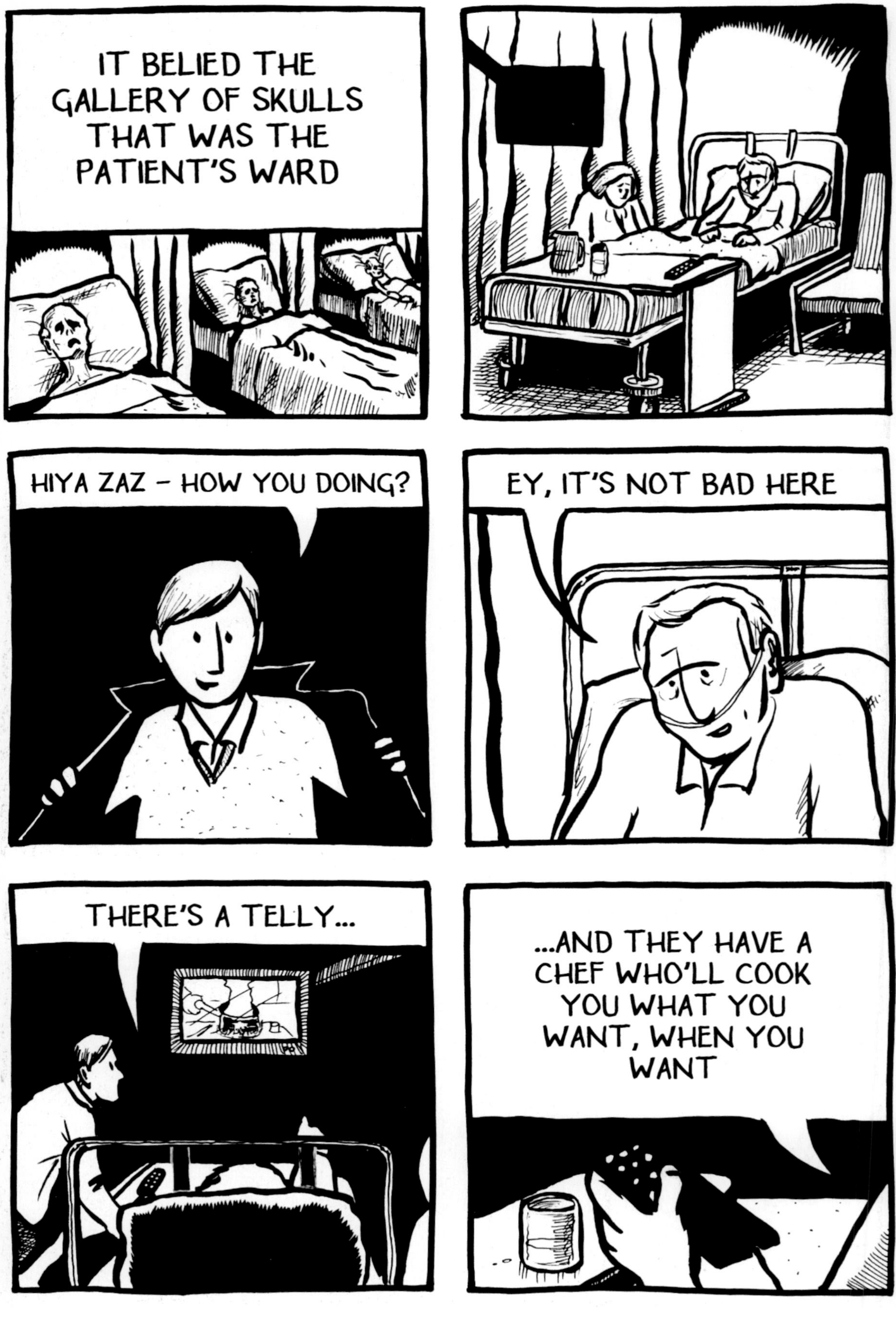
IT BELIED THE GALLERY OF SKULLS THAT WAS THE PATIENT'S WARD
HIYA ZAZ – HOW YOU DOING?
EY, IT'S NOT BAD HERE
THERE'S A TELLY...
...AND THEY HAVE A CHEF WHO'LL COOK YOU WHAT YOU WANT, WHEN YOU WANT

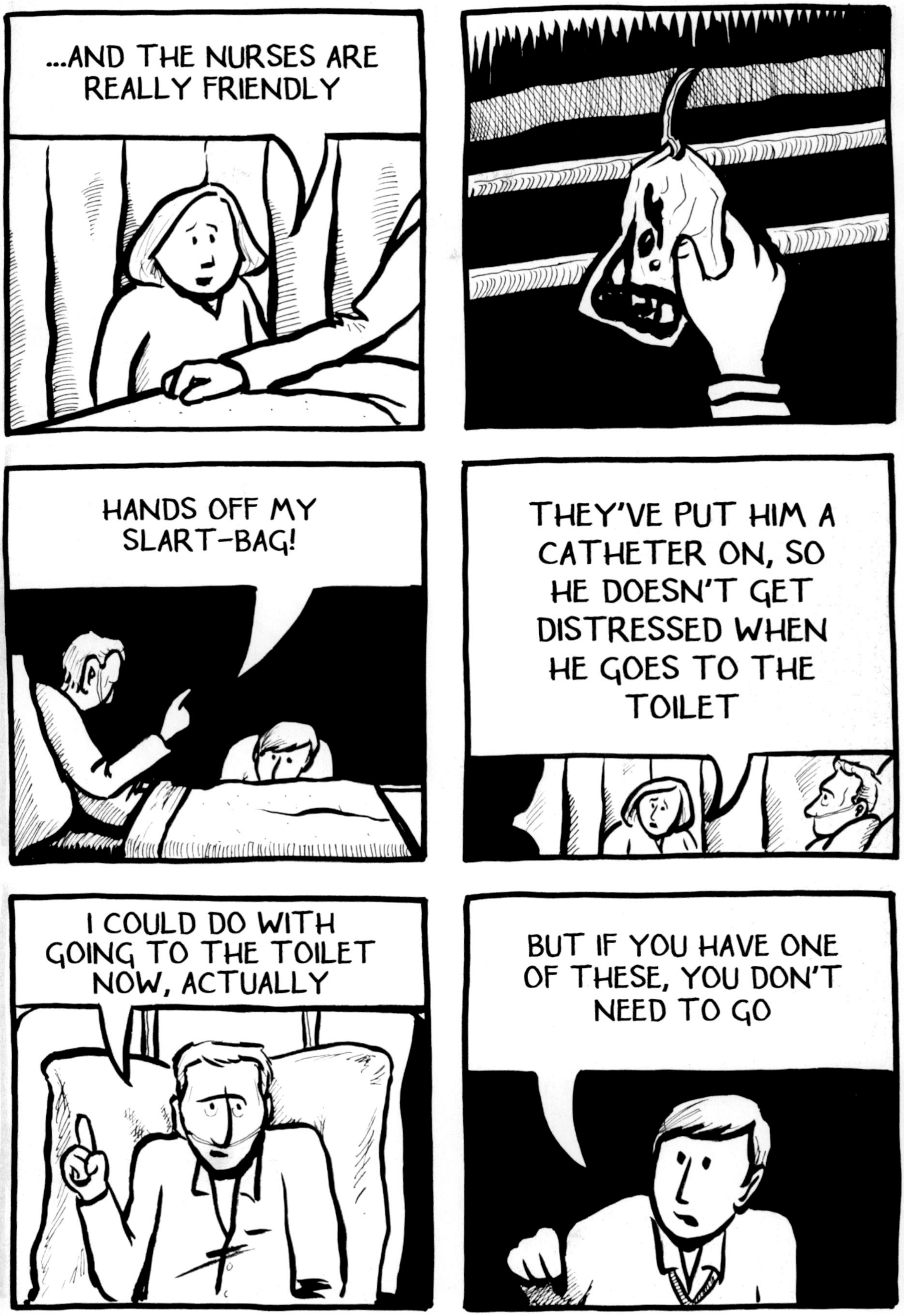
...AND THE NURSES ARE REALLY FRIENDLY
HANDS OFF MY SLART-BAG!
THEY'VE PUT HIM A CATHETER ON, SO HE DOESN'T GET DISTRESSED WHEN HE GOES TO THE TOILET
I COULD DO WITH GOING TO THE TOILET NOW, ACTUALLY
BUT IF YOU HAVE ONE OF THESE, YOU DON'T NEED TO GO

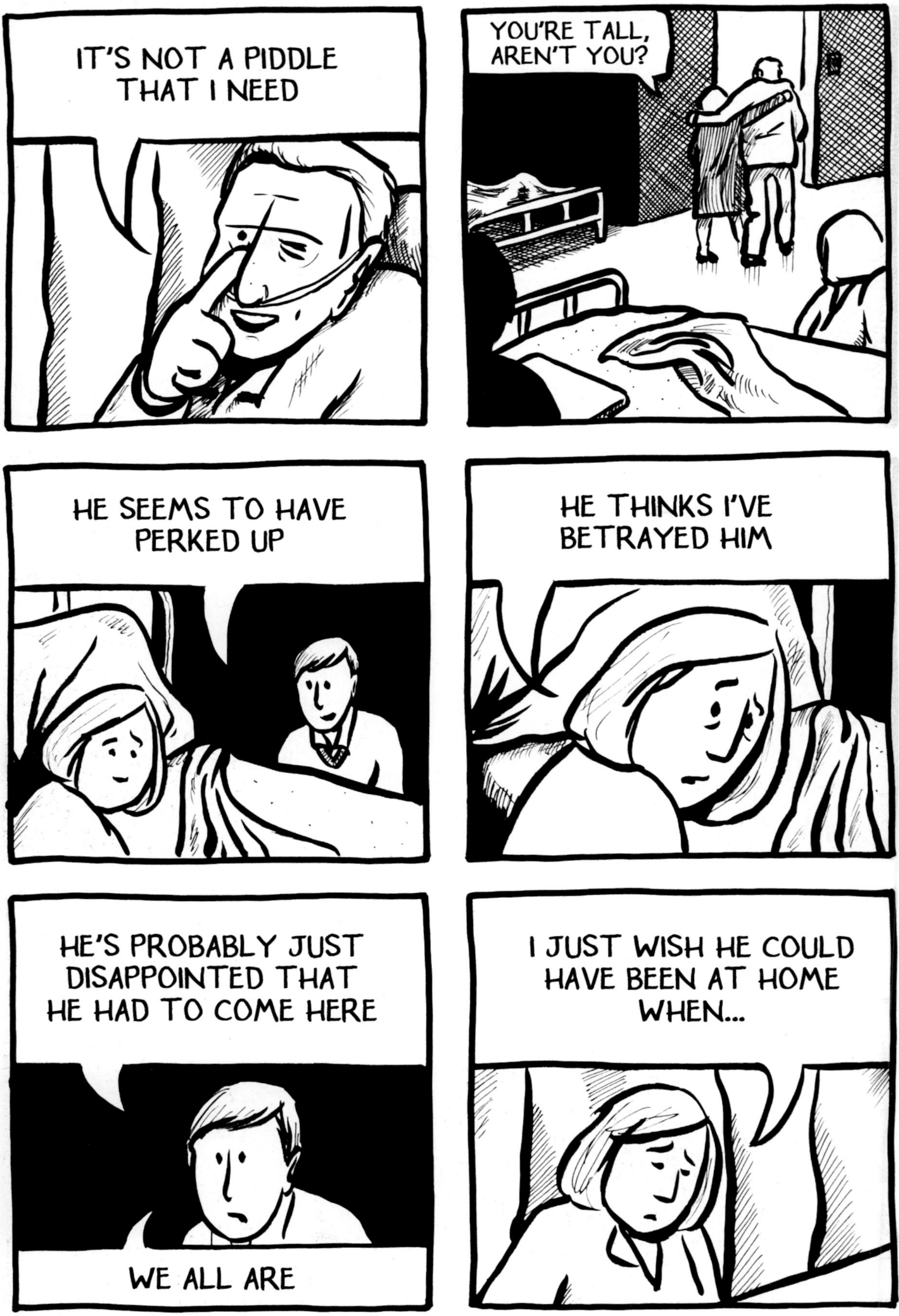
IT'S NOT A PIDDLE THAT I NEED
YOU'RE TALL, AREN'T YOU?
HE SEEMS TO HAVE PERKED UP
HE THINKS I'VE BETRAYED HIM
HE'S PROBABLY JUST DISAPPOINTED THAT HE HAD TO COME HERE
WE ALL ARE
I JUST WISH HE COULD HAVE BEEN AT HOME WHEN...

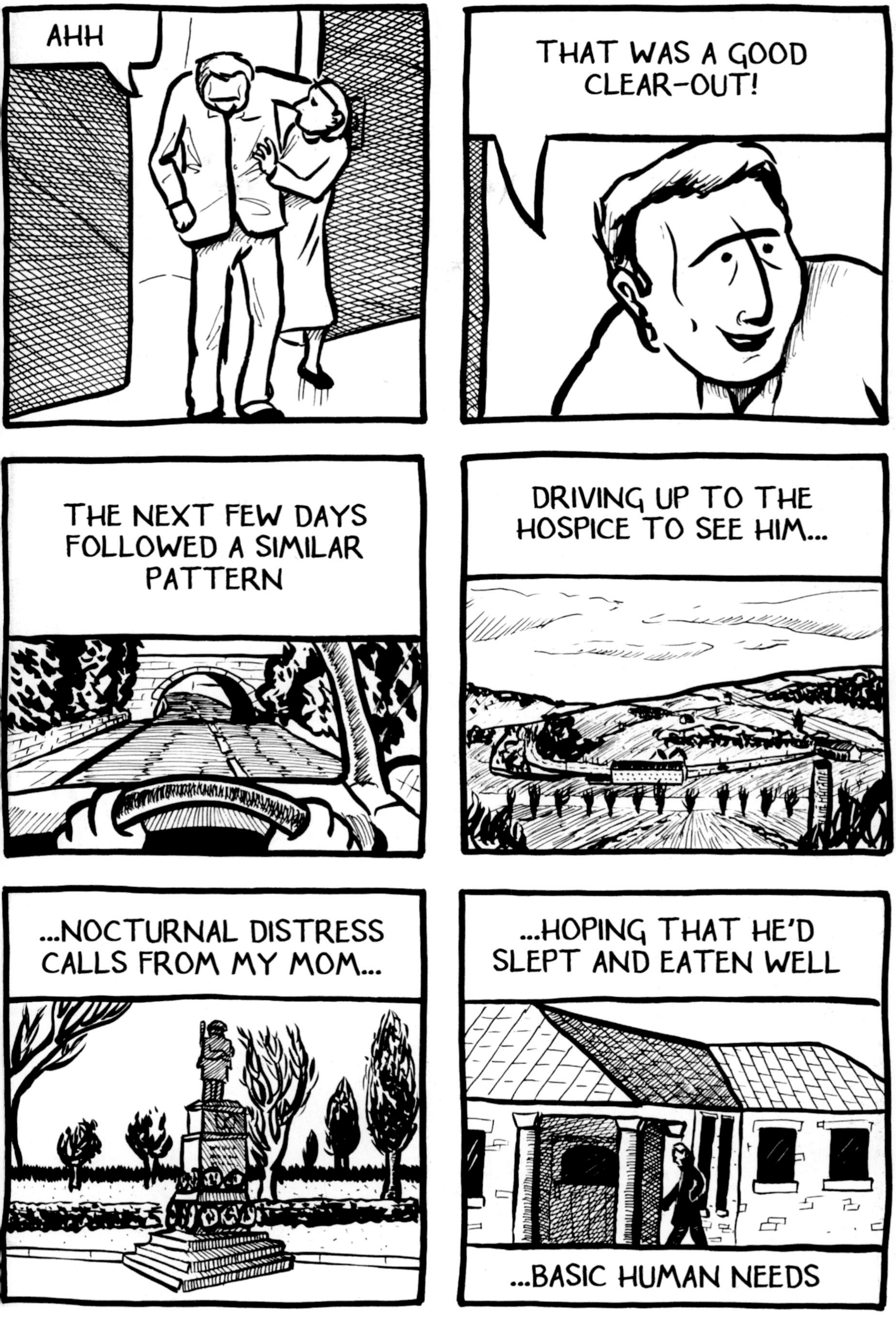
AHH
THAT WAS A GOOD CLEAR-OUT!
THE NEXT FEW DAYS FOLLOWED A SIMILAR PATTERN
DRIVING UP TO THE HOSPICE TO SEE HIM...
...NOCTURNAL DISTRESS CALLS FROM MY MOM...
...HOPING THAT HE'D SLEPT AND EATEN WELL
...BASIC HUMAN NEEDS

BUT ALTHOUGH HIS FOOD WAS REGURGITATED AND HE SLEPT FITFULLY...

...HE WAS ALWAYS PLEASED TO SEE ME

HOW YOU DOING?

NOT BAD. IRIS KEPT US UP ALL NIGHT

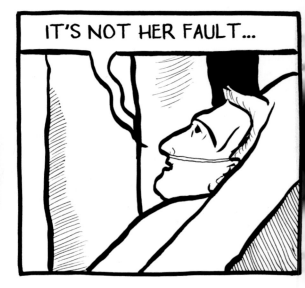

IT'S NOT HER FAULT...

...IT'S THE WAY SHE WAS BROUGHT UP

THE NURSE SAID YOU HAD DIARRHOEA YESTERDAY

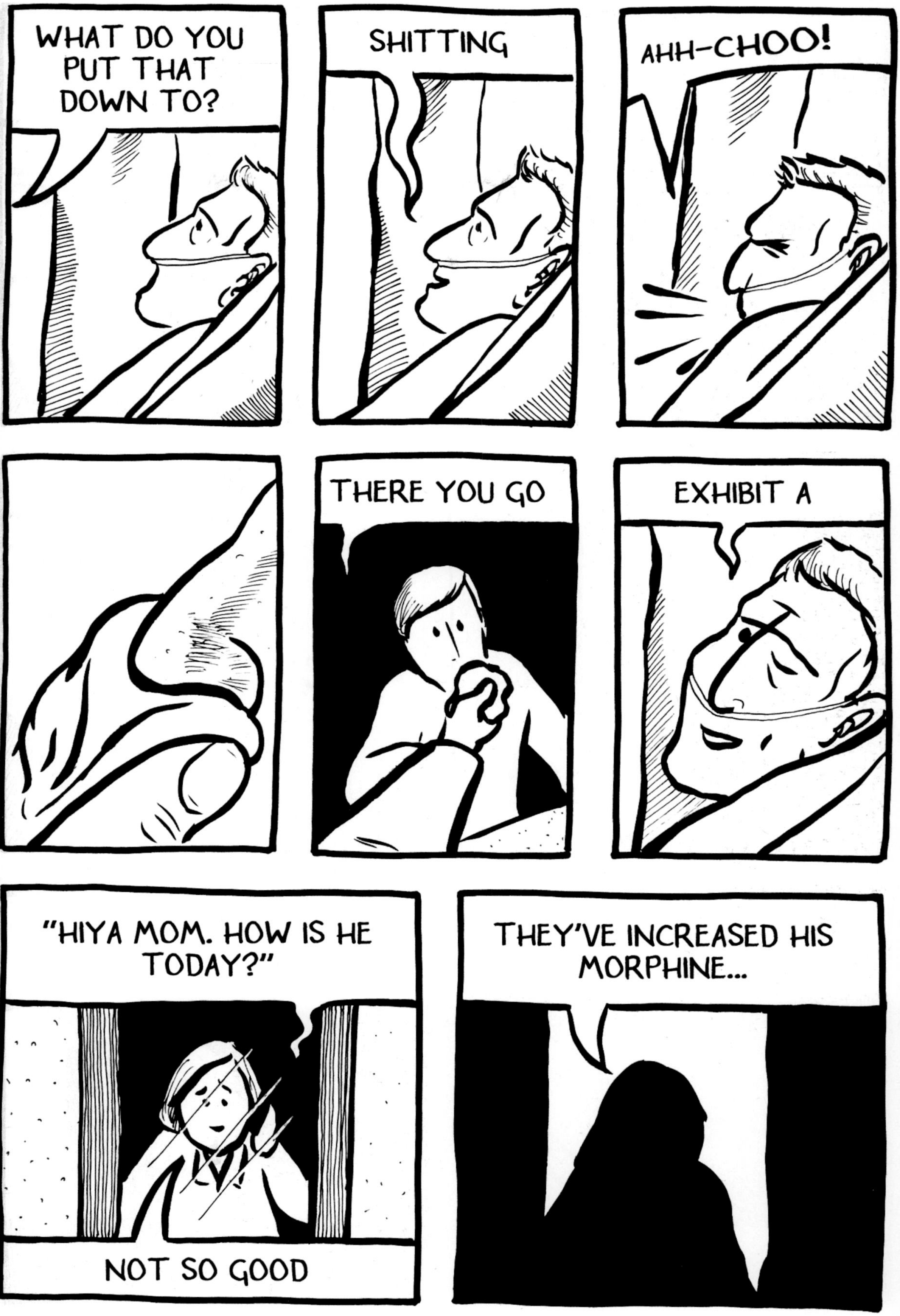

WHAT DO YOU PUT THAT DOWN TO?
SHITTING
AHH-CHOO!
THERE YOU GO
EXHIBIT A
"HIYA MOM. HOW IS HE TODAY?"
NOT SO GOOD
THEY'VE INCREASED HIS MORPHINE...

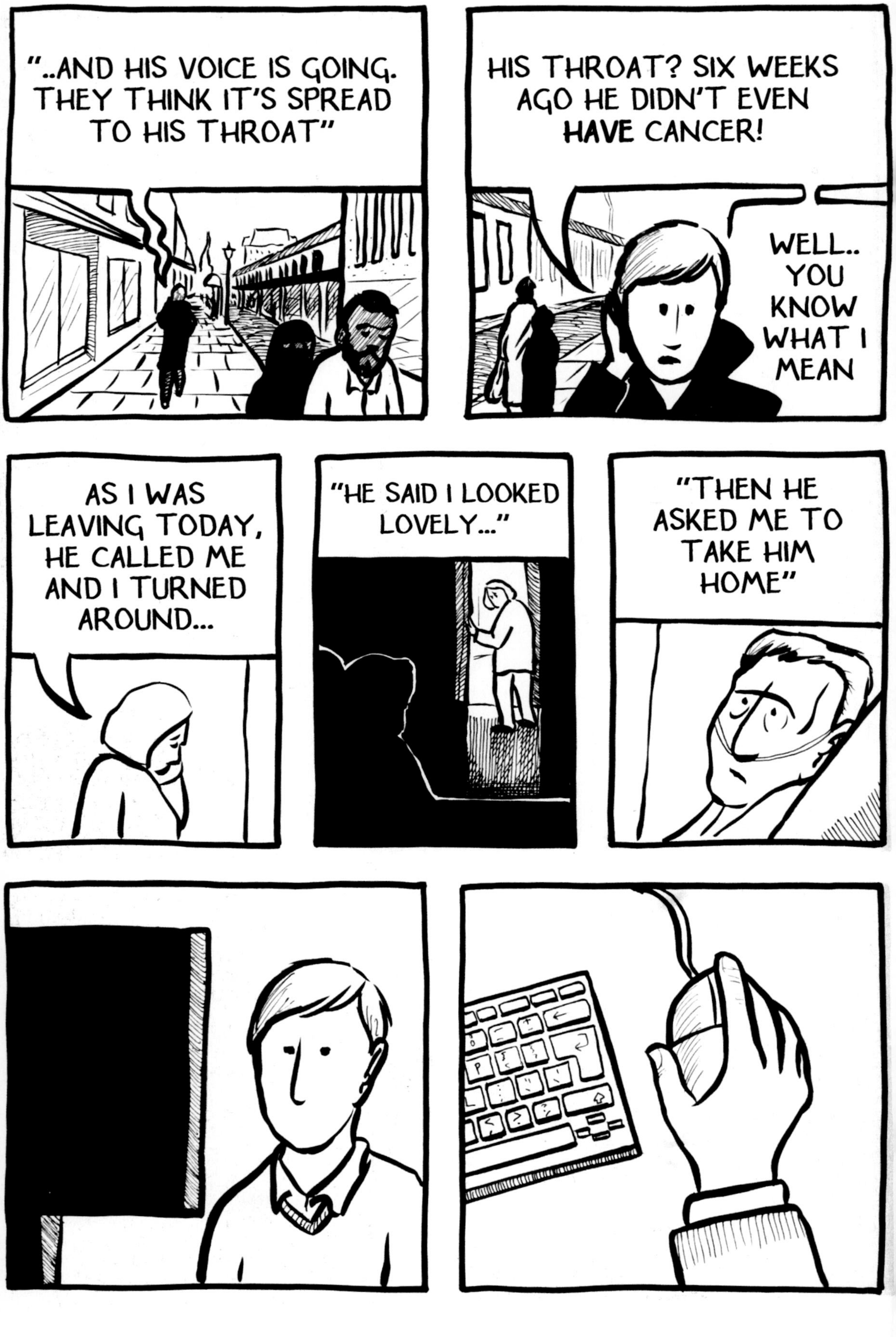
"..AND HIS VOICE IS GOING. THEY THINK IT'S SPREAD TO HIS THROAT"
HIS THROAT? SIX WEEKS AGO HE DIDN'T EVEN **HAVE** CANCER!
WELL.. YOU KNOW WHAT I MEAN
AS I WAS LEAVING TODAY, HE CALLED ME AND I TURNED AROUND...
"HE SAID I LOOKED LOVELY..."
"THEN HE ASKED ME TO TAKE HIM HOME"

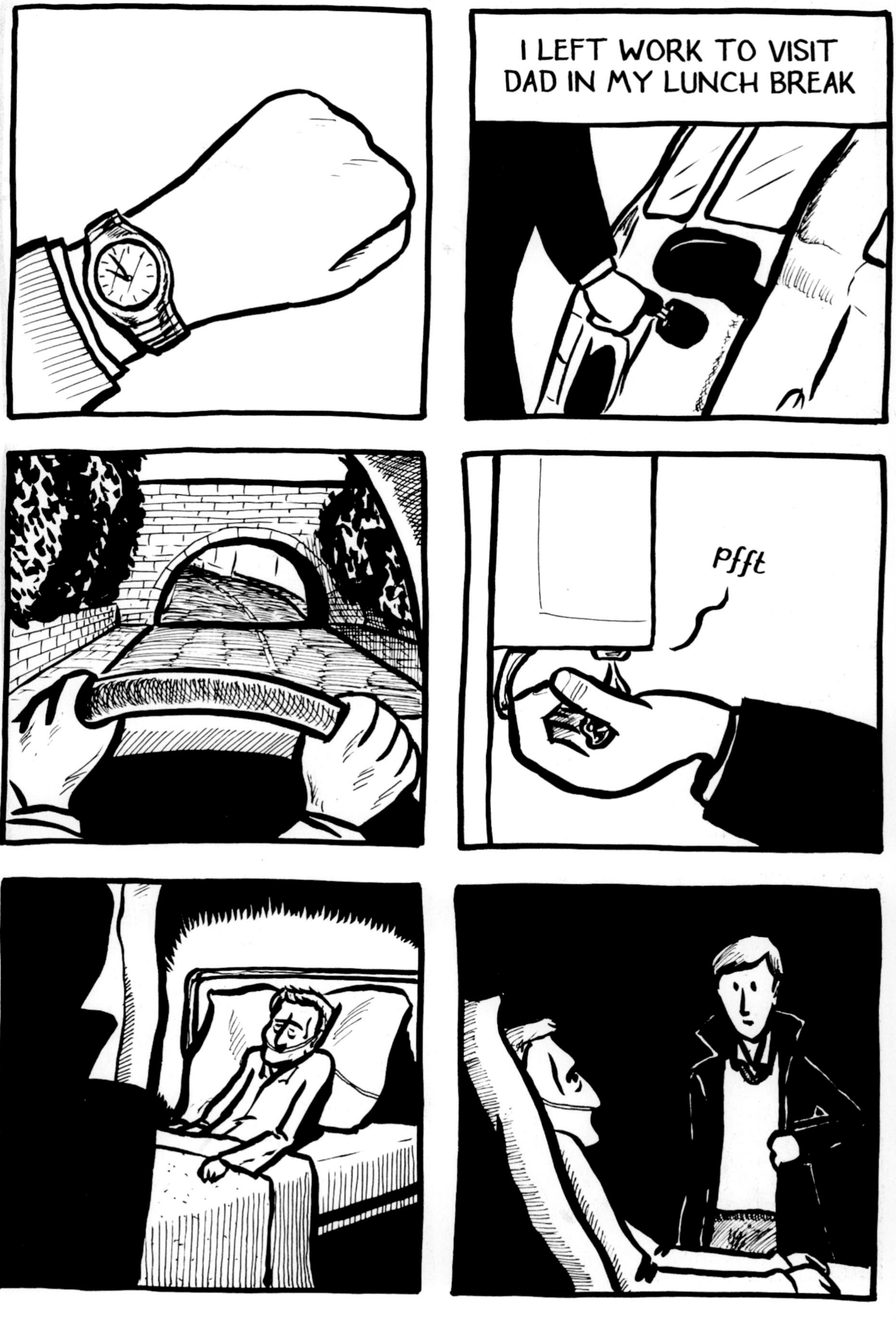
I LEFT WORK TO VISIT DAD IN MY LUNCH BREAK
pfft

Hiya Rosso
YOUR VOICE SOUNDS A BIT ROUGH
They said it's 'seeds', spread from my lungs
NOT ONLY WAS THE CANCER TAKING HIS BODY AWAY...
...IT WAS NOW STRANGLING HIS VOICE
THE ONLY PART OF HIM THAT WE HAD LEFT

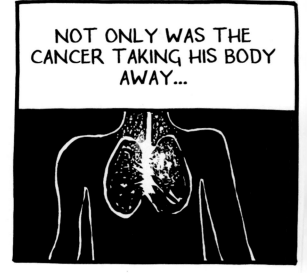

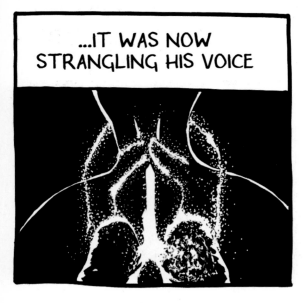

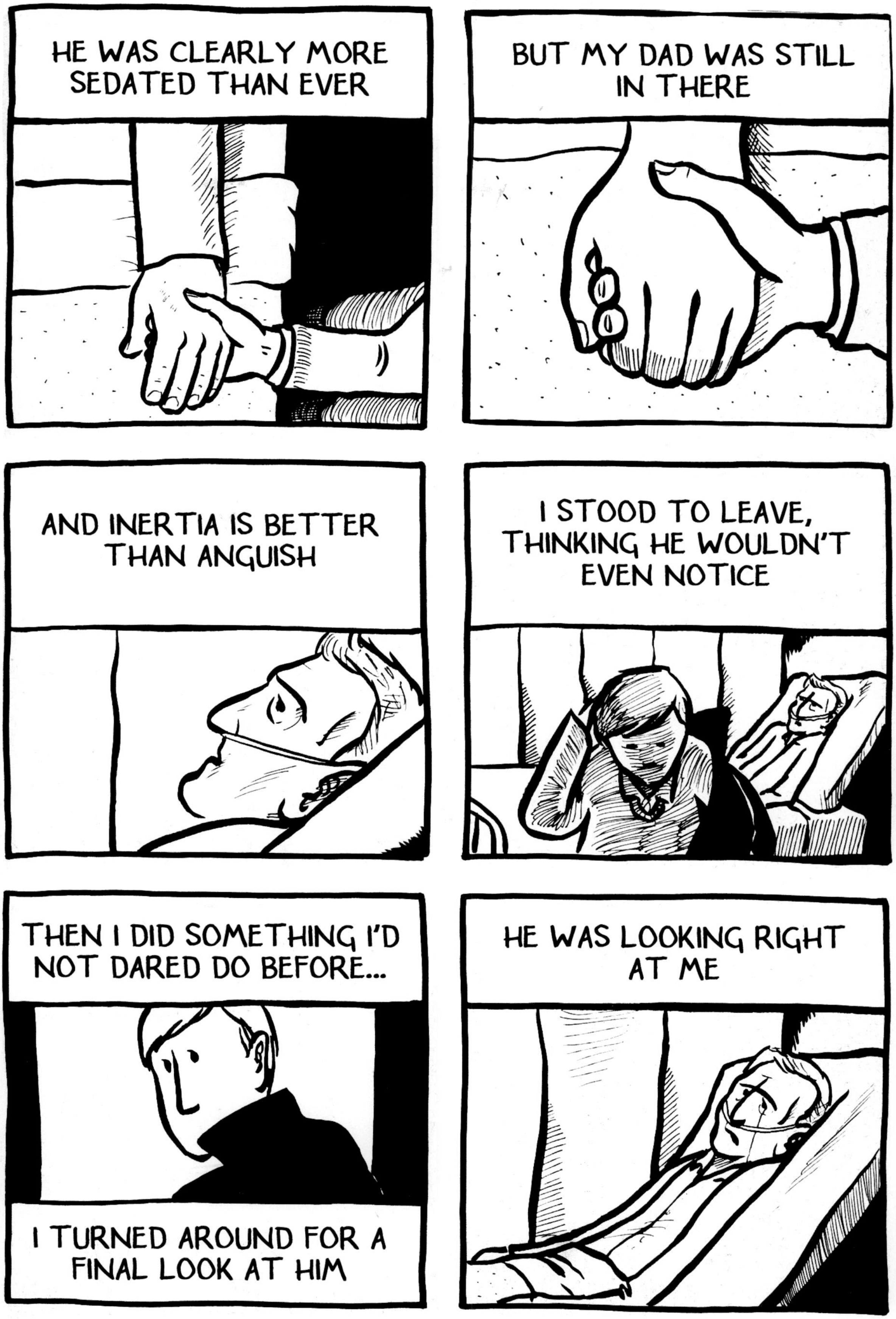
HE WAS CLEARLY MORE SEDATED THAN EVER
BUT MY DAD WAS STILL IN THERE
AND INERTIA IS BETTER THAN ANGUISH
I STOOD TO LEAVE, THINKING HE WOULDN'T EVEN NOTICE
THEN I DID SOMETHING I'D NOT DARED DO BEFORE...
I TURNED AROUND FOR A FINAL LOOK AT HIM
HE WAS LOOKING RIGHT AT ME

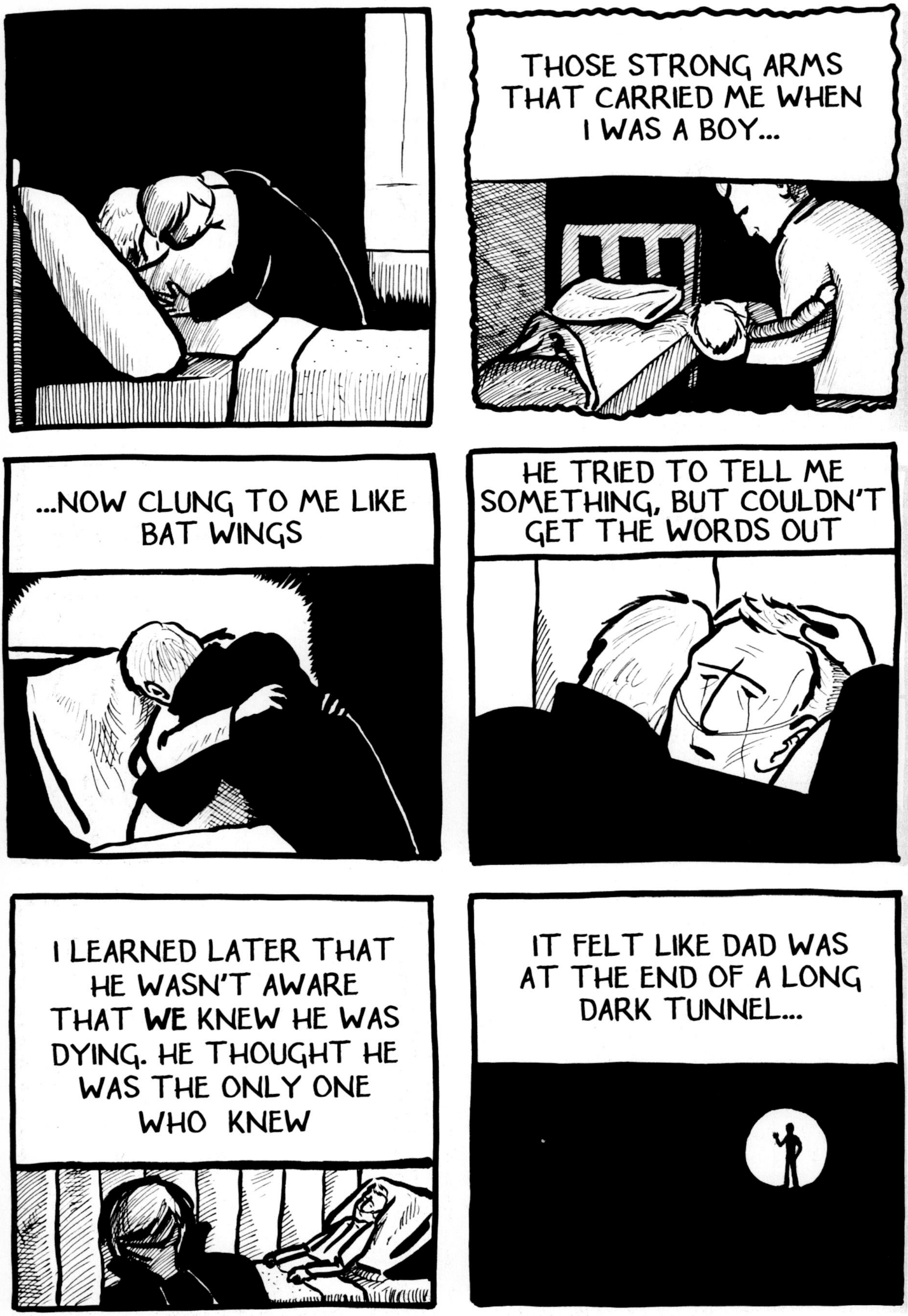
THOSE STRONG ARMS THAT CARRIED ME WHEN I WAS A BOY...
...NOW CLUNG TO ME LIKE BAT WINGS
HE TRIED TO TELL ME SOMETHING, BUT COULDN'T GET THE WORDS OUT
I LEARNED LATER THAT HE WASN'T AWARE THAT WE KNEW HE WAS DYING. HE THOUGHT HE WAS THE ONLY ONE WHO KNEW
IT FELT LIKE DAD WAS AT THE END OF A LONG DARK TUNNEL...

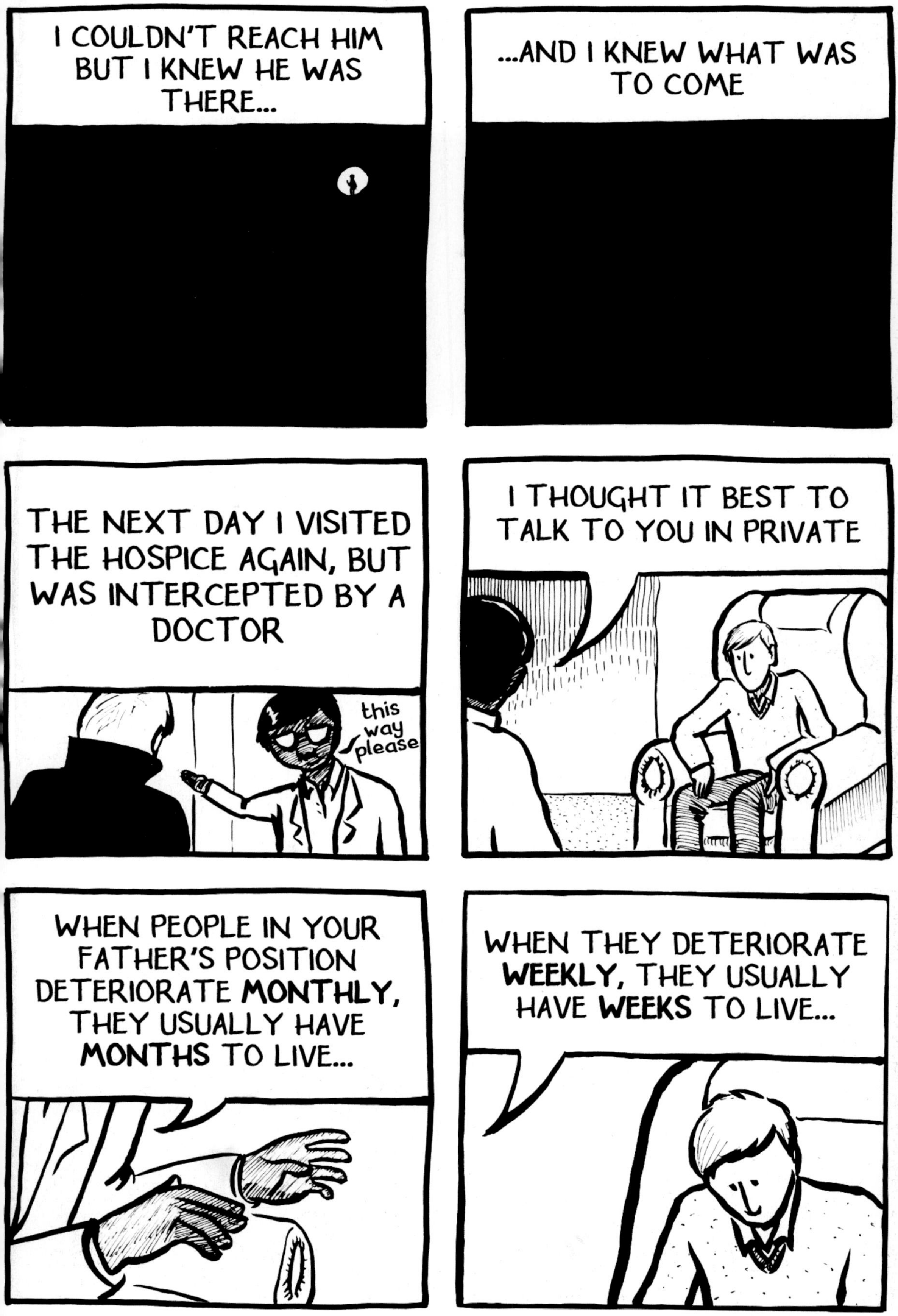

I COULDN'T REACH HIM BUT I KNEW HE WAS THERE...
...AND I KNEW WHAT WAS TO COME
THE NEXT DAY I VISITED THE HOSPICE AGAIN, BUT WAS INTERCEPTED BY A DOCTOR
this way please
I THOUGHT IT BEST TO TALK TO YOU IN PRIVATE
WHEN PEOPLE IN YOUR FATHER'S POSITION DETERIORATE **MONTHLY**, THEY USUALLY HAVE **MONTHS** TO LIVE...
WHEN THEY DETERIORATE **WEEKLY**, THEY USUALLY HAVE **WEEKS** TO LIVE...

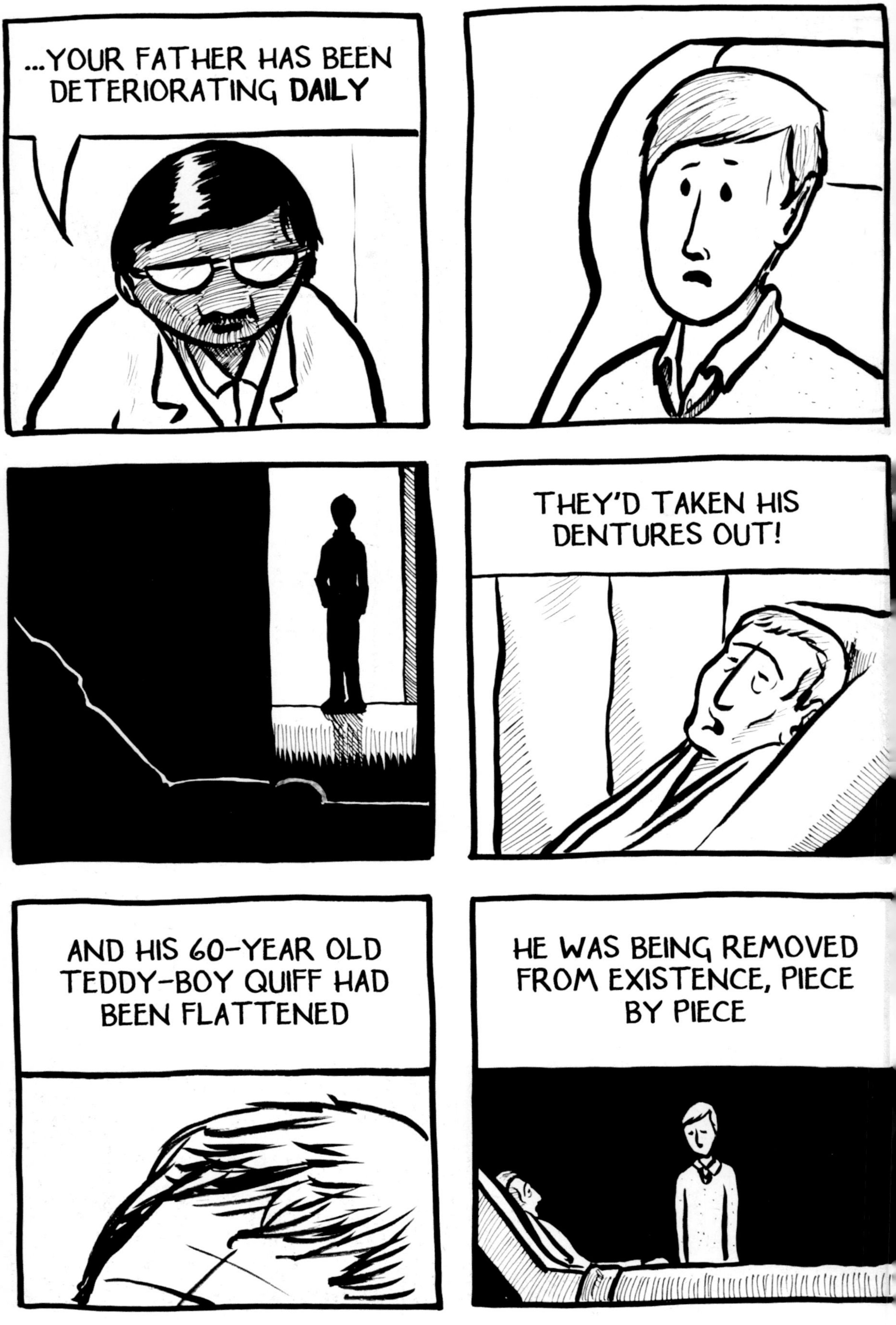
...YOUR FATHER HAS BEEN DETERIORATING **DAILY**
THEY'D TAKEN HIS DENTURES OUT!
AND HIS 60-YEAR OLD TEDDY-BOY QUIFF HAD BEEN FLATTENED
HE WAS BEING REMOVED FROM EXISTENCE, PIECE BY PIECE

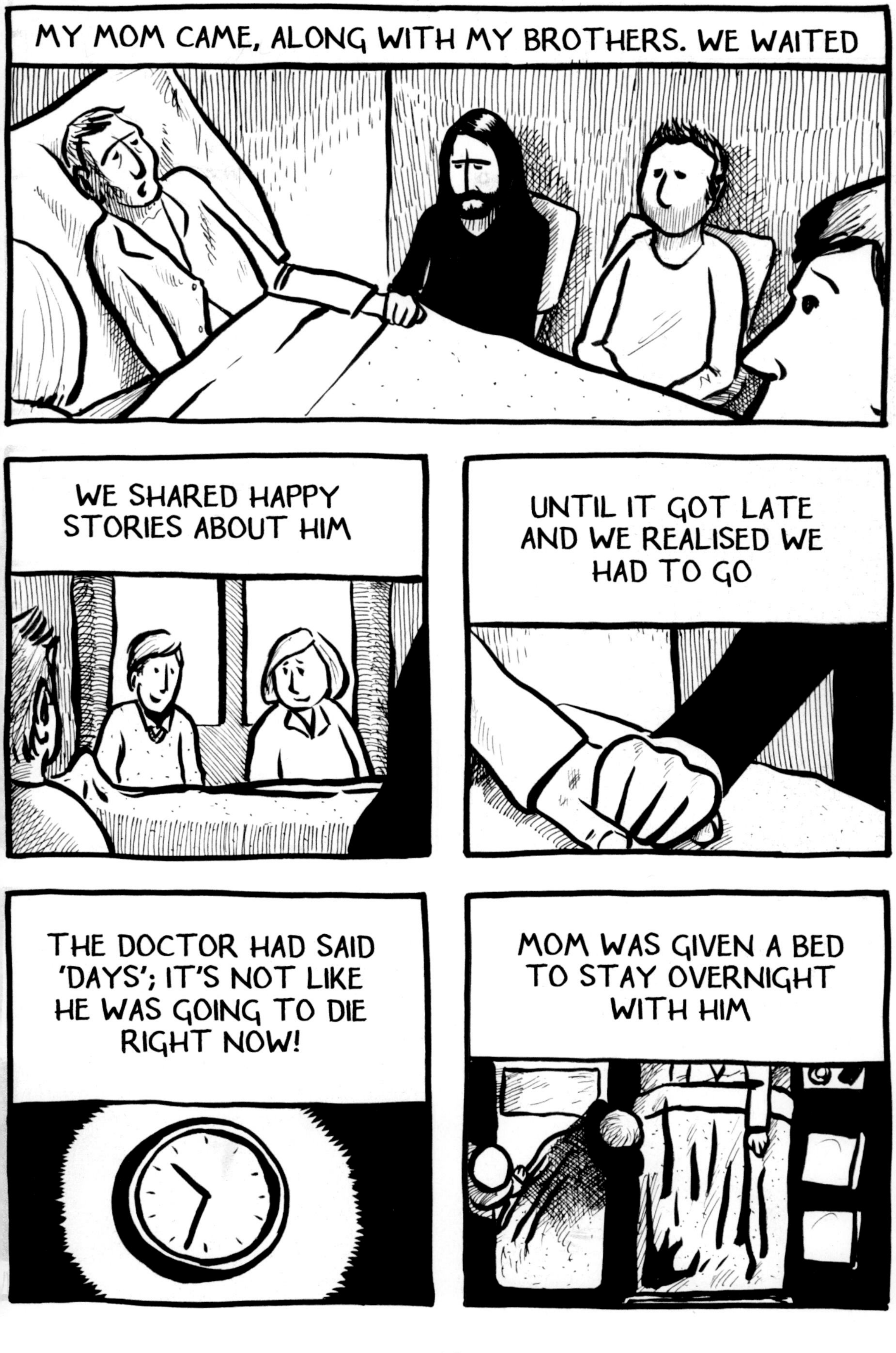
MY MOM CAME, ALONG WITH MY BROTHERS. WE WAITED
WE SHARED HAPPY STORIES ABOUT HIM
UNTIL IT GOT LATE AND WE REALISED WE HAD TO GO
THE DOCTOR HAD SAID 'DAYS'; IT'S NOT LIKE HE WAS GOING TO DIE RIGHT NOW!
MOM WAS GIVEN A BED TO STAY OVERNIGHT WITH HIM

BEFORE I LEFT I LEANED TO HUG DAD...

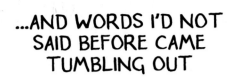

...AND WORDS I'D NOT SAID BEFORE CAME TUMBLING OUT

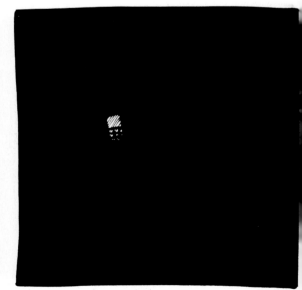

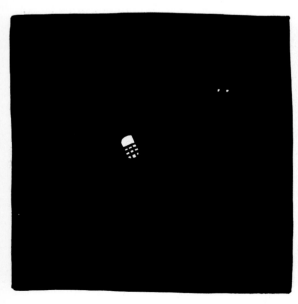

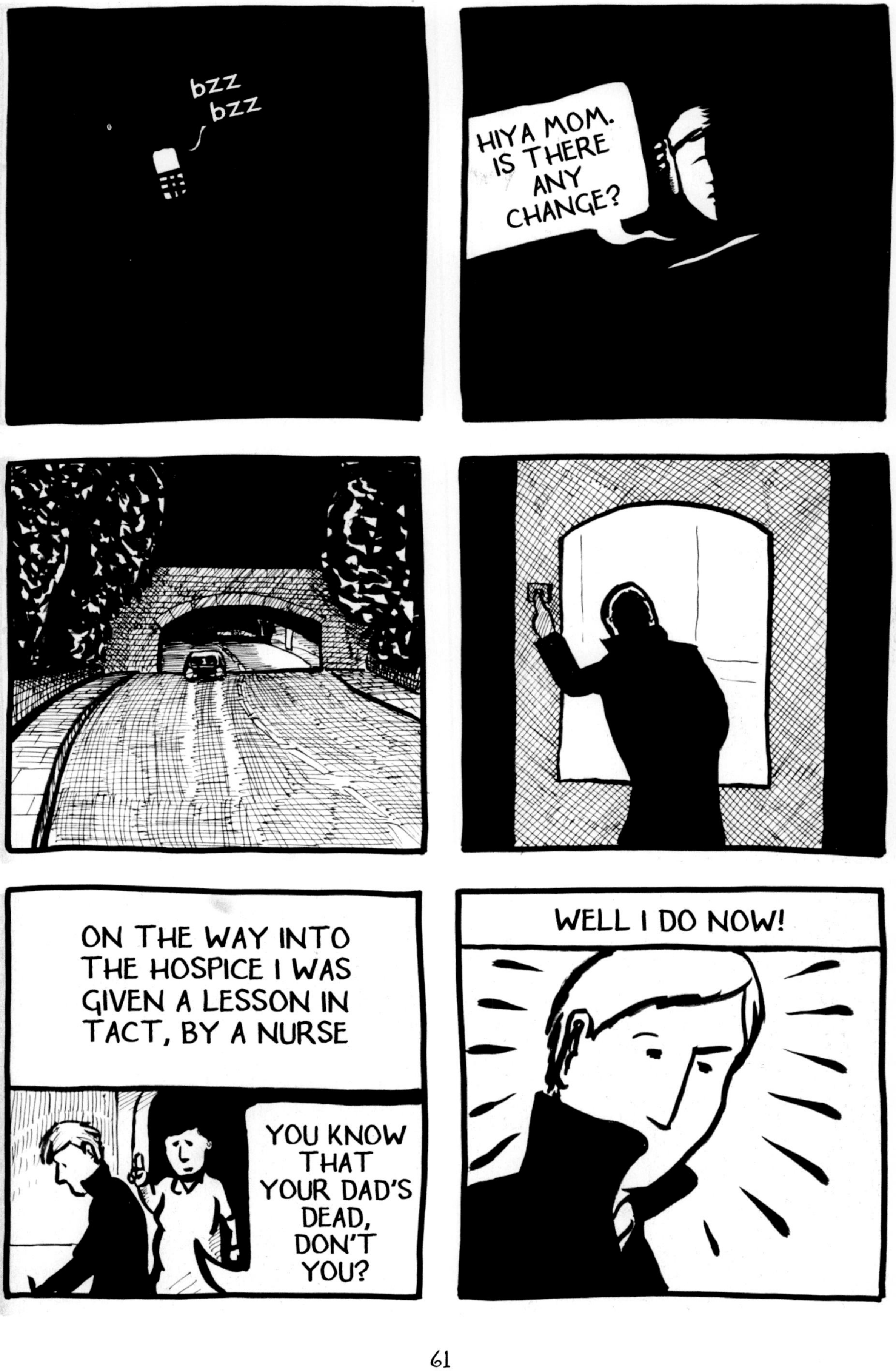
bzz
bzz
HIYA MOM. IS THERE ANY CHANGE?
ON THE WAY INTO THE HOSPICE I WAS GIVEN A LESSON IN TACT, BY A NURSE
YOU KNOW THAT YOUR DAD'S DEAD, DON'T YOU?
WELL I DO NOW!

**MOM AND MY BROTHERS WERE THERE**

**DAD WASN'T**

**WHEN CONFRONTED WITH A DEAD BODY THE EXPECTATION IS TO BE AFRAID**

**BUT THAT'S USUALLY ABOUT SOMEONE WE DON'T KNOW**

**THIS DEAD BODY BELONGED TO MY DAD**

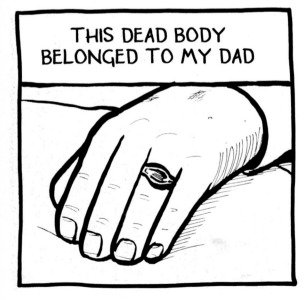

**I KNEW, HOWEVER, THAT I HAD TO ACCEPT THAT THIS WAS AN ARTEFACT, LIKE A CUT TOENAIL**

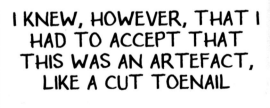

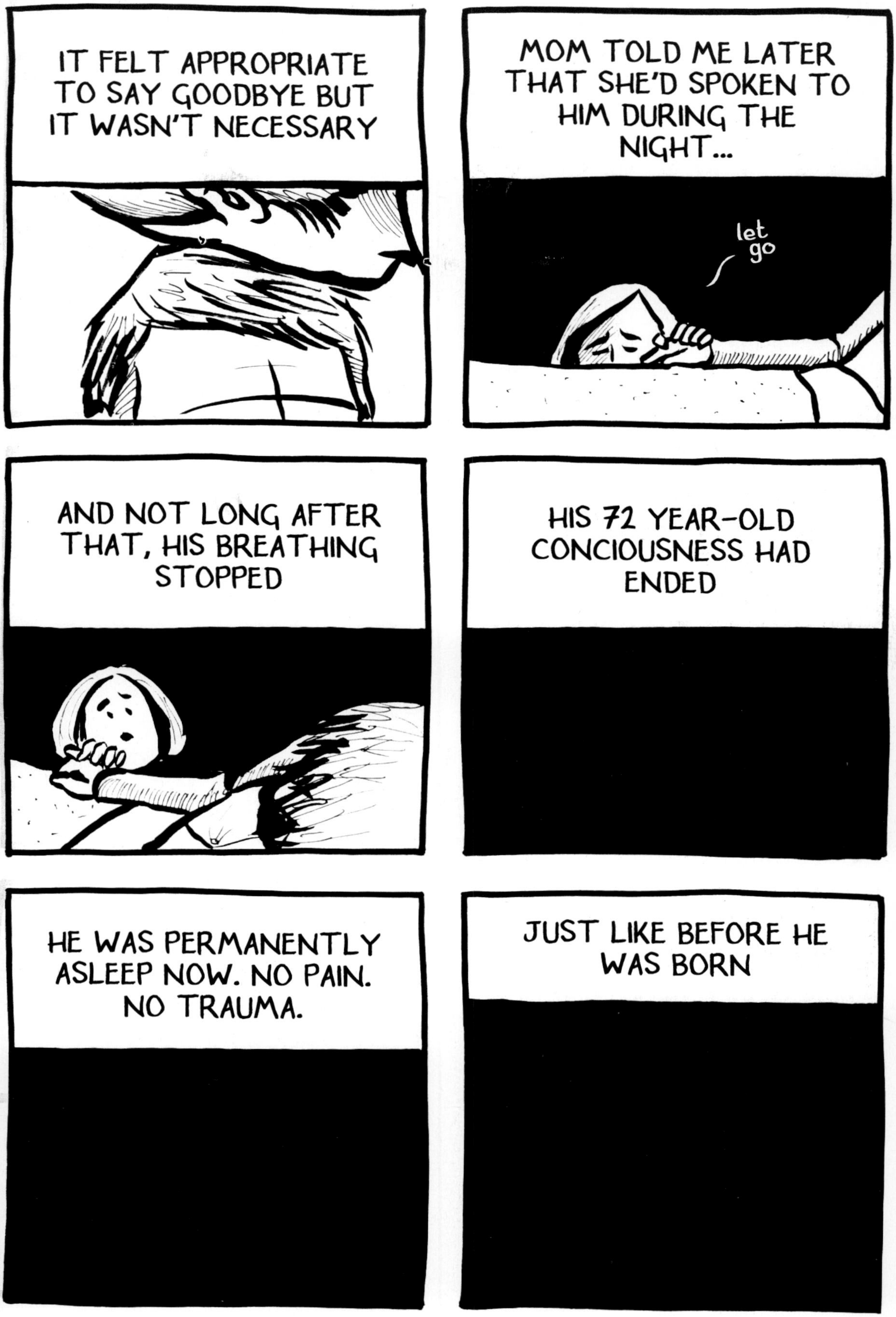
IT FELT APPROPRIATE TO SAY GOODBYE BUT IT WASN'T NECESSARY
MOM TOLD ME LATER THAT SHE'D SPOKEN TO HIM DURING THE NIGHT...
let go
AND NOT LONG AFTER THAT, HIS BREATHING STOPPED
HIS 72 YEAR-OLD CONCIOUSNESS HAD ENDED
HE WAS PERMANENTLY ASLEEP NOW. NO PAIN. NO TRAUMA.
JUST LIKE BEFORE HE WAS BORN

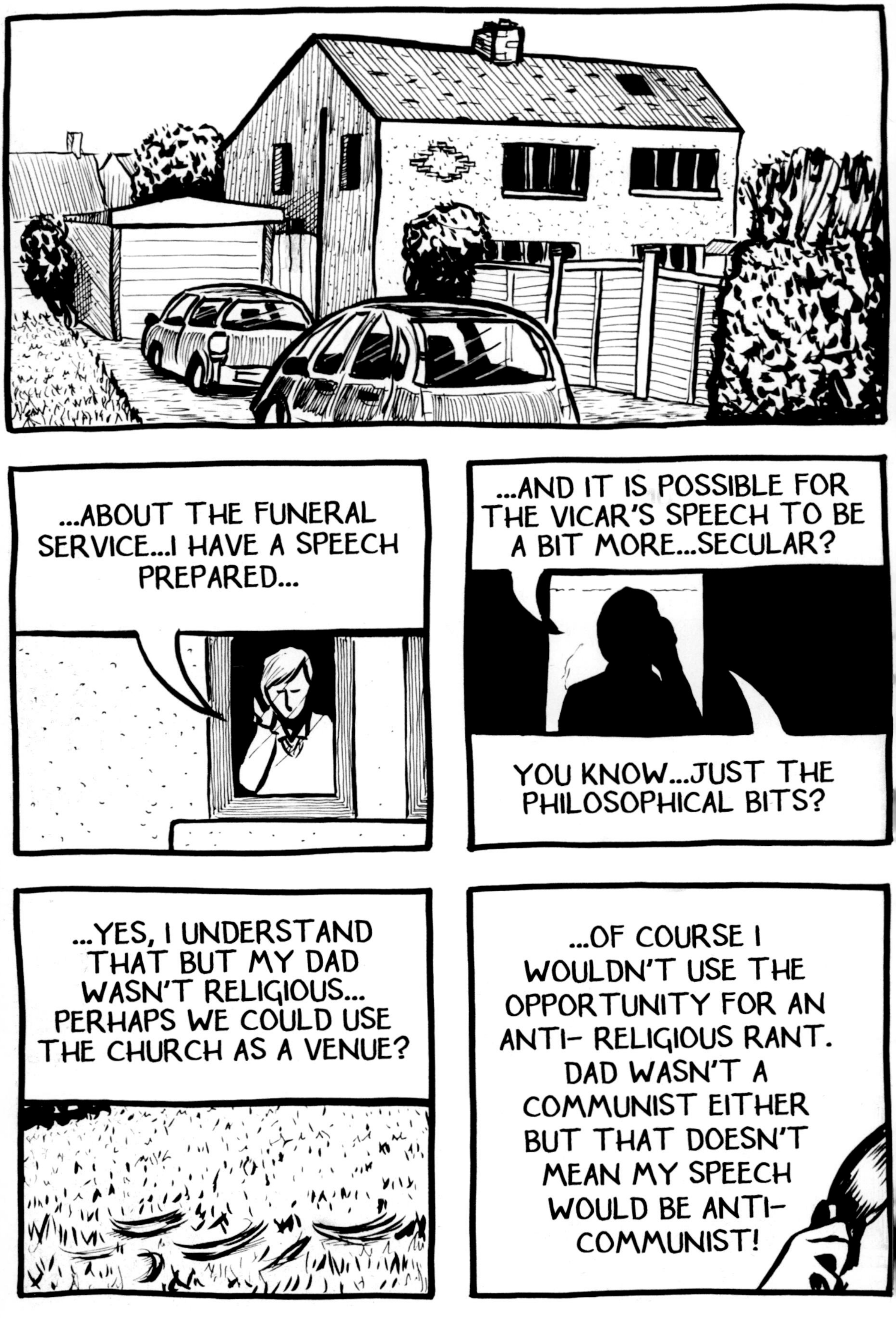
...ABOUT THE FUNERAL SERVICE...I HAVE A SPEECH PREPARED...
...AND IT IS POSSIBLE FOR THE VICAR'S SPEECH TO BE A BIT MORE...SECULAR?
YOU KNOW...JUST THE PHILOSOPHICAL BITS?
...YES, I UNDERSTAND THAT BUT MY DAD WASN'T RELIGIOUS... PERHAPS WE COULD USE THE CHURCH AS A VENUE?
...OF COURSE I WOULDN'T USE THE OPPORTUNITY FOR AN ANTI- RELIGIOUS RANT. DAD WASN'T A COMMUNIST EITHER BUT THAT DOESN'T MEAN MY SPEECH WOULD BE ANTI-COMMUNIST!

EVERYTHING ALRIGHT?

THE FUNERAL'S NEXT WEDNESDAY

AT THE FUNERAL I STARED AT THE COFFIN, HOPING IT MIGHT FEEL SIGNIFICANT...

...MENTALLY X-RAYING THE BOX IN ORDER TO STIMULATE EMOTION

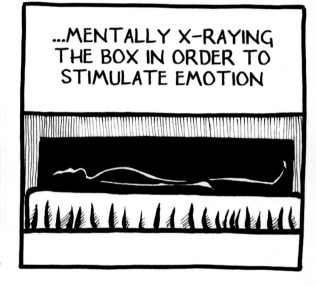

THIS WAS A WOODEN BOX, PRESENTED BY A STRANGER RECITING 2000 YEAR-OLD FABLES FROM THE MIDDLE EAST

IT HAD BECOME IRRELEVANT TO THE POINT OF SURREAL ; I'D SAID GOODBYE AT THE HOSPICE

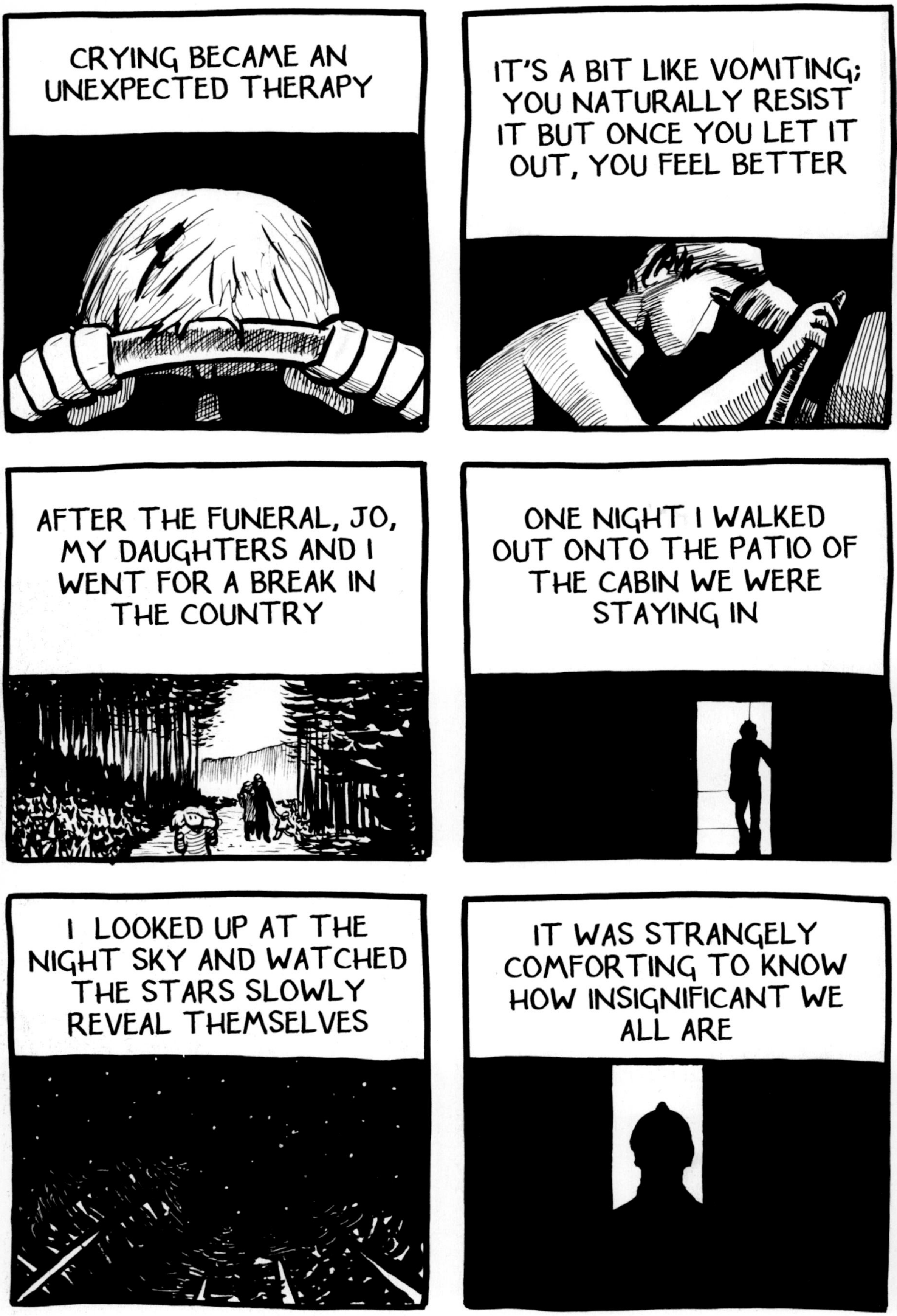
CRYING BECAME AN UNEXPECTED THERAPY
IT'S A BIT LIKE VOMITING; YOU NATURALLY RESIST IT BUT ONCE YOU LET IT OUT, YOU FEEL BETTER
AFTER THE FUNERAL, JO, MY DAUGHTERS AND I WENT FOR A BREAK IN THE COUNTRY
ONE NIGHT I WALKED OUT ONTO THE PATIO OF THE CABIN WE WERE STAYING IN
I LOOKED UP AT THE NIGHT SKY AND WATCHED THE STARS SLOWLY REVEAL THEMSELVES
IT WAS STRANGELY COMFORTING TO KNOW HOW INSIGNIFICANT WE ALL ARE

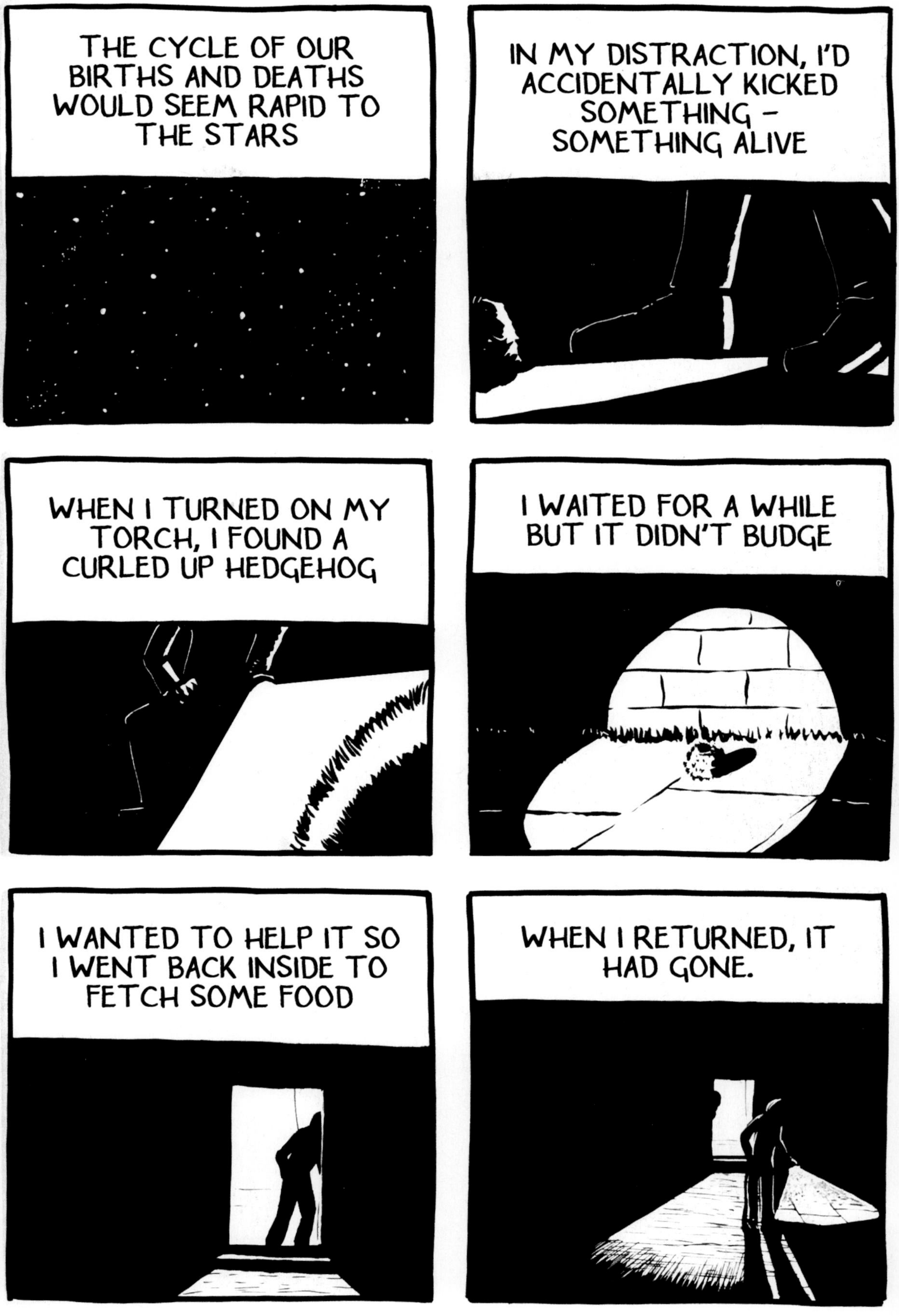
THE CYCLE OF OUR BIRTHS AND DEATHS WOULD SEEM RAPID TO THE STARS
IN MY DISTRACTION, I'D ACCIDENTALLY KICKED SOMETHING - SOMETHING ALIVE
WHEN I TURNED ON MY TORCH, I FOUND A CURLED UP HEDGEHOG
I WAITED FOR A WHILE BUT IT DIDN'T BUDGE
I WANTED TO HELP IT SO I WENT BACK INSIDE TO FETCH SOME FOOD
WHEN I RETURNED, IT HAD GONE.

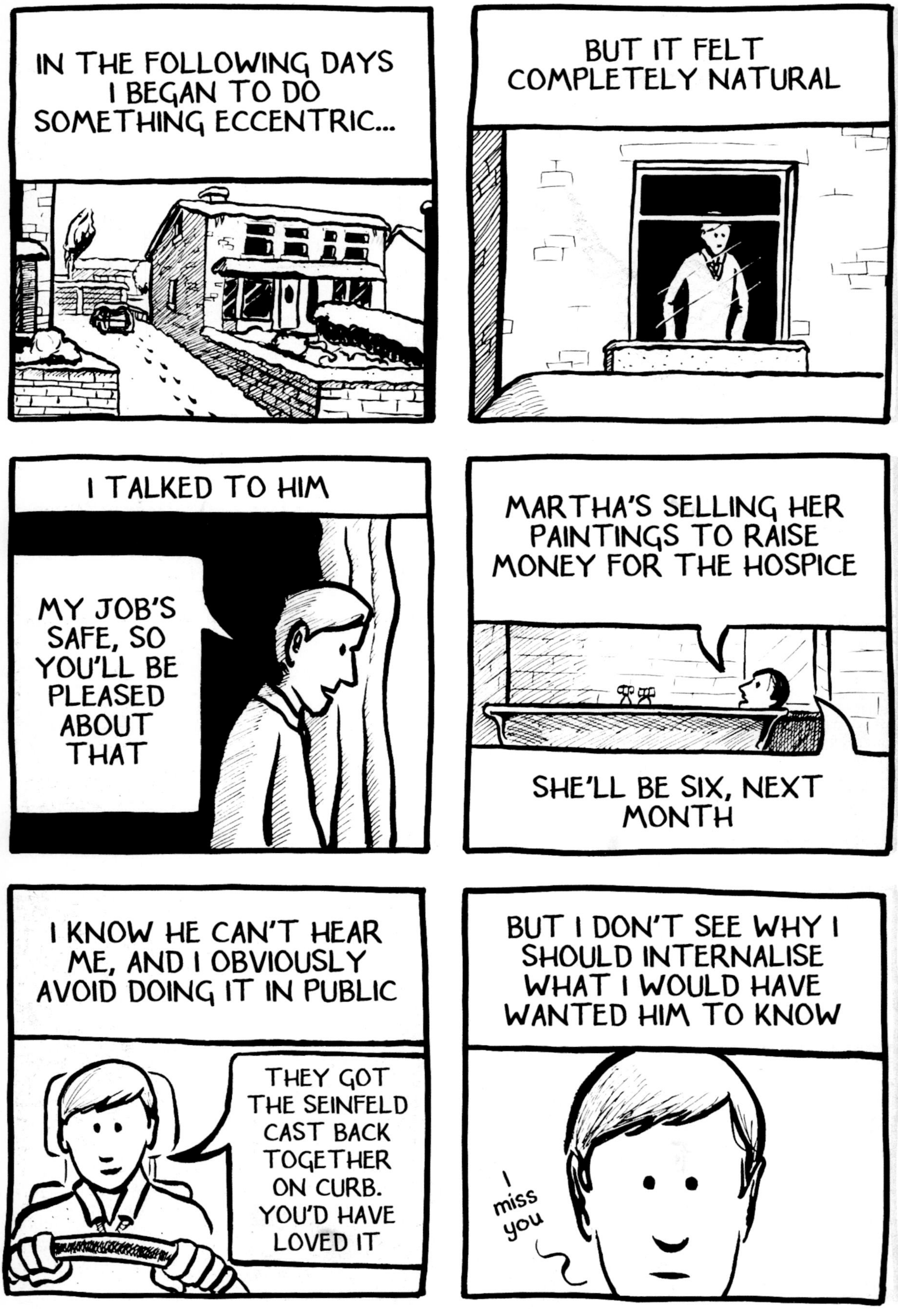
IN THE FOLLOWING DAYS I BEGAN TO DO SOMETHING ECCENTRIC...
BUT IT FELT COMPLETELY NATURAL
I TALKED TO HIM
MY JOB'S SAFE, SO YOU'LL BE PLEASED ABOUT THAT
MARTHA'S SELLING HER PAINTINGS TO RAISE MONEY FOR THE HOSPICE
SHE'LL BE SIX, NEXT MONTH
I KNOW HE CAN'T HEAR ME, AND I OBVIOUSLY AVOID DOING IT IN PUBLIC
THEY GOT THE SEINFELD CAST BACK TOGETHER ON CURB. YOU'D HAVE LOVED IT
BUT I DON'T SEE WHY I SHOULD INTERNALISE WHAT I WOULD HAVE WANTED HIM TO KNOW
I miss you

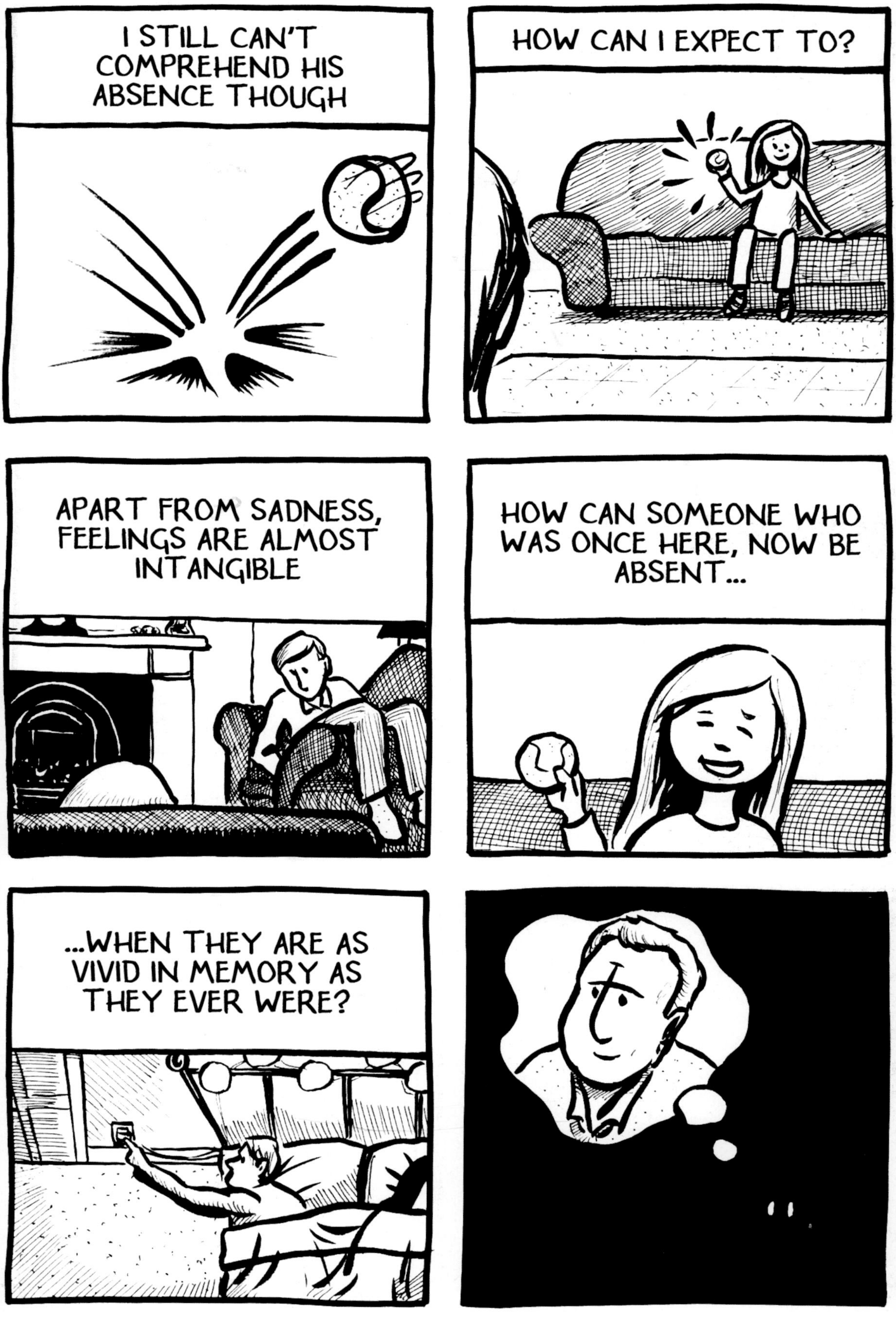
I STILL CAN'T COMPREHEND HIS ABSENCE THOUGH
HOW CAN I EXPECT TO?
APART FROM SADNESS, FEELINGS ARE ALMOST INTANGIBLE
HOW CAN SOMEONE WHO WAS ONCE HERE, NOW BE ABSENT...
...WHEN THEY ARE AS VIVID IN MEMORY AS THEY EVER WERE?

THE END

# ABOUT THE AUTHOR

Having spent a decade as a graphic designer, pushing a mouse around a desk, Ross Mackintosh decided it was time to return to the craft of drawing.

Being influenced by artists such as Adrian Tomine, Marjane Satrapi, Craig Thompson and Alison Bechdel, Ross wanted to inject some real life into black and white pictures. He didn't realise his inspiration would come quite so suddenly.

"As a child growing up in the UK, I couldn't help but find escapism in American culture. For others it was sport and TV, for me it was movies and comics.

Even though my tastes moved from superhero to independents, it's a gratifying retreat to immerse myself within the pages and connect with the author's story.

It's enlightening to learn that someone else is having the same thoughts and experiences as you."

'Seeds' is his first graphic novel.

Ross Mackintosh lives in Yorkshire, UK.